FROM THE JUDAISM OF JESUS TO THE CHRISTIANITY OF PAUL

IGOR P. LIPOVSKY

American Academy Press
Washington D.C.

AMERICAN ACADEMY PRESS

FROM THE JUDAISM OF JESUS TO THE CHRISTIANITY OF PAUL.
Copyright © 2022 by Igor P. Lipovsky.

Scripture quotations are taken from the Holy Bible New International Version,
copyright 1984, 2011. International Bible Society.

Printed and bound in the United States of America

FIRST EDITION.

Library of Congress Cataloging-in-Publication Data

Lipovsky, Igor P., 1950–
From the Judaism of Jesus to the Christianity of Paul / Igor P. Lipovsky
p. cm.
Includes bibliographical references and index.
1. Christianity—Origin. 2. Jesus Christ—Teachings. 3. Paul, the
Apostle, Saint. 4. Bible. N.T.—Criticism, interpretation, etc.
5. Church history—Primitive and early church, ca.30-600. I. Title.

ON THE COVER: First Christians. Fresco. Catacombs of Domitilla, Rome, 2nd
century C.E.

ISBN: 978-0-578-37614-1

Library of Congress Control Number: 2022903001

American Academy Press

For my mother,
Nina Lipovskaya (Robinson),
with love

Acknowledgments

FIRST OF ALL I would like to thank the American Academy of Arts and Sciences, whose support and generous contribution made this book possible.

I owe a huge debt of gratitude to my insightful friends and colleagues from the Department of Religion at Yale and from the Divinity School at Duke. They graciously read the manuscript in its final stages and offered many helpful suggestions.

My deep appreciation goes to my editor Edward M. Levy. Thanks to his perceptive insights and editorial skill, my book has been immeasurably improved.

Contents

Introduction

JESUS'S MISSION TOOK PLACE at the beginning of the Common Era. At this time, the Jewish people were in a tense spiritual state, awaiting the coming of the Messiah—the messenger of God, who, according to the biblical prophecies, was to save his people from the rule of pagan foreigners and restore David's kingdom. Messianic hopes had begun to fill Judea's religious and spiritual life ever since Pompey's legions invaded the country in 63 BCE and transformed the sovereign Judean kingdom into a country dependent on Rome. Popular leaders, such as Judas the Galilean, called upon the Jews not to submit to the pagan newcomers, as having cognized the true God, they must serve only the Lord. The Romans, fearing the appearance of new Maccabees, at first left Judea its own rulers and complete religious freedom. However, being governed by pagans was so humiliating for Jewish monotheists that almost all the years of Roman rule were accompanied by unrest and uprisings—especially in the north of the country, in Galilee. The appearance of John the Baptist, and later of Jesus himself, led to an explosion of messianic emotions in Judea and frightened the Roman authorities. After all, the Messiah, according to the then dominant belief, would expel the foreigners and sit on the throne of David—that is, become the Judean king. Fear of this coming king and of the people who followed him forced Pontius Pilate, the Roman procurator, to condemn Jesus to crucifixion, even without the decision of the supreme religious court (Sanhedrin), which was never called. The people waited, believing that the all-powerful Jesus, having become famous for his miracles, would reduce the Romans to ashes and restore the Judean kingdom. But Christ turned out to be a Messiah of a totally different kind: He came not to rule the people but to save their souls for the other, main world—the kingdom of God. The fact that Jesus did not ruin his enemies but instead suffered from them himself greatly contradicted the biblical

1

prophecies and led to a split within the Jewish people. While the majority remained loyal to the traditional notions of the Savior, a minority who believed in Jesus founded Christian communities and began to preach the idea of the one God of Israel and his Messiah among the peoples of the Greco-Roman world. Thus, by the end of the first century, a new religion, Christianity, had grown out of Judaism.

To this day, the mistaken point of view—that Christianity, as an independent religion, was founded by Jesus and his disciples—is widespread. In reality, the teachings of Jesus and his closest followers—the apostles Peter, John, and James—were merely a new direction of Judaism. The true founding fathers of Christianity were people who never knew Jesus—the apostles Paul, Barnabas, and Silas, and the evangelist Luke, and John the Evangelist. While Christ's disciples represented only one of the trends of Judaism, supporters of the apostle Paul left Judaism altogether, creating a completely new religion. According to the viewpoints of Jesus's disciples, one should accept Judaism in order to become a Christian. A non-Jew could not be a Christian—this belief prevailed in all Christian communities till the '70s of the first century. It is not surprising that the pagan, Greco-Roman world viewed Christianity as merely one of the trends of Judaism.

The apostle Paul was the first to rebel against this approach to the believers in Jesus, and in his preaching to Gentiles and even Jews, he called upon them not to follow the laws of Judaism. Why did Paul, a faithful Jew who meticulously observed the customs and traditions of his ancestors, consider it possible to free the believers in Jesus from the uneasy burden of Moses's laws? First, from his experience of being a missionary, Paul had reached the conclusion that as long as Christian preachers insist on circumcision, observance of the Sabbath, and kashrut laws, their preaching will prove ineffective. The numerous, difficult-to-follow laws of Moses, especially the demand of male circumcision, generally scared away pagans who wanted to connect with the true God and his Messiah. Second, Paul was convinced that the resurrection of Jesus was itself firm evidence that he was the Messiah the Jewish people awaited. And since the true Messiah is above any of the Mosaic laws, absolute faith in him frees one from the laws of Judaism, which had to be followed only before his arrival. If the first coming of the Messiah—thought Paul—replaced the laws of Judaism with faith in Jesus, then his second coming will mean the end of our world: the apocalypse and Christ's judgment of the people.

2

Paul's idea—the rejection of all Jewish customs, rituals, and traditions in order to connect pagans to monotheism—proved to be incredibly fruitful. The Greco-Roman world was ready to embrace Jewish monotheism but only in a "clean state" without the national and historical Jewish dress. Paul's preaching of the Savior and his resurrection became the link that united Jewish monotheism with Hellenistic culture.

The disciples of Jesus, on the one hand, and Paul, on the other, represented two different views of the nature of Christ and the path his adherents had to follow. While Peter, John, and James regarded Jesus as "Son of Man" and the Savior of the Jewish people, Paul and his supporters saw in Jesus the "Son of God" and the Savior of all peoples. While the disciples of Jesus firmly stood on the ground of Judaism, Paul believed that faith in Jesus alone should replace all the laws of Judaism. Certainly, the version of Christianity that Jesus's disciples preached was unappealing to Gentiles but could, with time, be adopted by the majority of Jews. On the other hand, the version suggested by Paul was attractive to pagans but unacceptable to the Jews. These different interpretations of Christianity are reflected in the four canonical gospels: Mark and Matthew represent the position of Jesus's disciples, while Luke and John the Evangelist mirror the vision of the apostle Paul.

It should be remembered that the gospels are not a chronological account of Christ's earthly life and preaching but rather are works of literature about him. Nor were the authors of the gospels part of the circle of Jesus's disciples; indeed, they were not even Jesus's contemporaries. The canonical gospels were created 40 to 70 years after his crucifixion based on different and, at times, contradictory testimonies of those who knew Jesus and heard his preaching. This fact explains many of the inconsistencies and variations between the four gospels. Unfortunately, we do not have the original texts for any of them. The earliest known complete copies are from the fourth century, the result of the efforts of several previous generations of copyists. Unlike the Middle Ages, when copying New Testament literature was done by monks—the second-and-third-century fathers of the Church repeatedly complained about the insolence of copyists, who allowed themselves to edit New Testament works. Although the process of canonization of the gospels of Matthew, Mark, Luke, and John had already begun in the second century, the copyists' alterations and their impunity from consequences continued to the fourth century, when the Church finalized the New Testament. From this point on, editing the sacred texts was considered a crime.

What then did the first copyists change? First of all, they removed from the texts all anti-Roman statements, of which there must have been many; after all, Jesus and his disciples lived and preached mostly in Galilee, which was the epicenter of Jewish opposition to Rome. According to the Gospel of Matthew, Jesus's infancy coincided with the death of Herod the Great (4 BCE) and the transition of power to the latter's son, Archelaus. At this time, the Judean kingdom, especially its northern part, Galilee, was the arena of widespread uprisings against the Romans and local Judean authorities, who were appointed by Rome. Notably, the Gospel of Matthew mentions the escape of Mary and Joseph with the baby to Egypt, from where they returned only after the unrest in the country subsided. Archelaus was confirmed ruler of Judea, while Galilee was given to Herod's other son, Antipas. But anti-Roman opposition did not stop.

When Jesus was around ten years of age (6 CE), a revolt of the Zealots—fighters for the freedom of Judea—flared up in his native Galilee. At the head of the rebellion was Judas the Galilean, whose entire family (father, sons, and grandsons), over the course of nearly a century, pushed Galilee to resist Rome's rule. The Zealots freed most of Galilee, including Jesus's native town—Nazareth. And though the Roman legions crushed this revolt, the Zealots did not retire their weapons. They went to difficult-to-access mountainous regions and from there continued a partisan war against the Romans. In those times, the Zealots were everywhere, even in Jesus's close circle. It is known that at least one of the twelve disciples of Jesus, Simon, from the town of Cana, took part in the Zealot movement—that is why he was called "the Zealot." Fifteen years after the crucifixion of Jesus, Galilee again revolted against the rule of Rome, and after another twenty years, at the beginning of the Jewish War (66–73 CE), it became the main place of battle with the Roman army. At a time when the lands of Galilee were suffering under Roman occupation, Jesus could not but encounter the pain and anger of his people; he must have talked about this with his disciples, especially since one of them was a Zealot.

What happened to all the anti-Roman episodes in the gospels, three of which—Mark, Matthew, and John—were written by Jews? They were completely removed or emasculated by the first copyists, as any criticism of the Romans could bring harm to the Christian communities in the empire. Moreover, the copyists themselves, being Romans and Hellenes, felt offended by the anti-Roman rhetoric of the Jews. In Galilee, like nowhere else in Palestine, there prevailed strong anti-Roman sentiments—an outright hatred toward Roman and Hellenistic pagans. It manifested itself everywhere and in everything. For instance, three to four miles from ancient Nazareth was the large Hellenistic city of Sepphoris. However, none of the gospels says a word about this important Hellenistic center in Galilee, yet they mention cities and towns that are much smaller and located farther away, such as Capernaum, Bethsaida, Cana, and the even more distant Bithynia and Emmaus, near Jerusalem. This was explained by the outright enmity that existed between Jewish monotheists and Hellenistic pagans. The latter, taking advantage of the support of the Roman garrison, demonstratively disregarded the traditions of Jewish monotheism and frequently provoked the Jews to clash with them. It was not by chance that Jesus and his disciples never went to their nearest pagan neighbors and had no relationship with them. This mutual alienation manifested itself in the most fatal way when the first copyists from among former pagans began to "improve" the gospels: on the one hand, removing anti-Roman statements, and on the other, making anti-Jewish additions, falsely depicting Christ as being opposed to the Judeans, and the Judeans to Christ. The copyists' efforts to whitewash the Romans and demonize the Jews proved to be so successful that the blame for the crucifixion of Jesus was transferred from the procurator Pontius Pilate to the Jews.

The texts of the gospels were changing for another reason as well—so that heretical movements could not take advantage of them. But the victory of one or another point of view in early Christianity was determined not so much by theological arguments and discussions as by the numerical strength and political and economic influence of each community. At first, the most numerous and authoritative community was considered to be Jerusalem's church in Judea, which was headed by the apostles Peter and James (Jesus's brother). The leadership of Jerusalem's church adhered to the position of the apostle Peter, which did not go beyond the bounds of Judaism. However, after the Romans' destruction of Jerusalem and the Temple in 70 CE and the death of many Jewish Christians, the influential Roman community became the most authoritative. In second place were the Christian communities of Continental and Asiatic Greece. All of them embraced the apostle Paul's point of view, which already represented a new religion. It was the Roman and Greek churches that, in the end, decided who among the Christians held "true" or "heretical" positions.

$\smallsmile\!\!\!\approx\!\!\!\smallsmile$

The Jewish Messiah

"I am the gate; whoever enters through
me will be saved." (John 10:9)

Bethlehem or Nazareth?

Where did Jesus come from? However strange it may seem, there is no definitive answer to this question. Of the four canonical gospels, two—Mark and John—are completely silent on the matter; the other two—Matthew and Luke—have differing answers. According to Matthew, Joseph and Mary had always lived in their native Bethlehem, and it was fear of King Herod, and later of his son Archelaus, that forced them to flee first to Egypt and then to Nazareth. The gospel of Luke indicates clearly that Nazareth was the homeland of Jesus's parents; yet, it also specifies that at the time of the baby's delivery, Mary and her husband were in Bethlehem. But the gospel makes no mention of any escape to Egypt. So why is it that two gospels are silent on the issue while the other two give far from identical versions of Jesus's birth and infancy? This is explained by understanding the audiences for whom the evangelists wrote: the gospels of Mark and John were initially meant for the Gentiles, particularly Greco-Roman pagans. For them, it did not matter where and in what Judean city the Messiah (*Christ* in Greek) was born. They had little interest in knowing the place and even circumstances of Jesus's birth. The Jews, however, had a very different attitude to this. According

7

to biblical prophets, the Messiah— "God's Anointed" and the Savior of the people of Israel—would be born in Bethlehem, in the homeland of King David and necessarily descend from King David's line. This is why Matthew, who primarily addressed the Jews in his gospel, places Jesus's birth in Bethlehem and mentions his direct descent from King David. Moreover, Matthew went further: Knowing how the Jews revered Moses, he described Jesus's birth in a way that would most resemble the circumstances of Moses's birth in Egypt. Thus, Herod's slaughter of the infants is incredibly reminiscent of the pharaoh's murder of newly born Jewish boys. The escape and later return of the holy family from Egypt would have called to mind not only the journey Moses made but the words of the biblical prophecy that the Savior was to come from Egypt. In this way, Jesus, according to Matthew, was not only the Messiah whom the Jewish people awaited but a second Moses, who came to save Israel. Nothing of the sort is said by Mark or John. Could they, having narrated so much of Jesus's life and preaching, really have not known anything about the circumstances of his birth? Evidently, their silence on this testifies not only to the fact that their Greco-Roman audience did not need such details but also to their unwillingness to repeat a version in which they themselves did not believe and, most importantly, one they did not consider necessary for spreading faith in Jesus. However, in order not to interfere with the Jews' bonding to Jesus, Mark and John did not state anything that would contradict the version supported by Matthew. Notably, the apostle Paul likewise did not say anything of the place and circumstances of Jesus's birth, despite the fact that his letters are the earliest New Testament writings.

Luke took a different position. He intended his gospel for everyone, both Jews and Gentiles. Naturally, he too deemed it necessary to indicate Bethlehem as Christ's birthplace, as well as emphasize that Jesus descended from the line of King David. But Luke, unlike Matthew, does not mention the holy family's escape to Egypt and, most importantly, admits that Jesus's parents came not from ancient Judean Bethlehem but from unremarkable Galilean Nazareth and that they happened to be in Bethlehem by chance. It is likely that the Bethlehem version of Jesus's birth appeared and spread quickly only because all the first Christians were Jews. However, this version also had such great literary merit that Gentiles, who later began to dominate in Christian communities, gladly accepted it, even though they, unlike the Jews, were not in need of it. The fact that the gospels of Mark and John—just as the works of the apostle

Paul—ignore the Bethlehem version suggests that Jesus not only spent his years of infancy and youth in Nazareth but was also born there.

From the Holy Spirit or from man?

While locating Jesus's birth in Bethlehem appeared under the direct influence of biblical prophecies about the Messiah, the idea of his birth from the Holy Spirit is more confusing and complex. In the Old Testament, there is only one rather unclear prediction by the prophet Isaiah regarding this: "The virgin will conceive and give birth to a son, and will call him Immanuel" (Isaiah 7:14). Admittedly, it is unlikely that the idea of conception by the Holy Spirit would have arisen on the basis of this prophecy alone, which can be interpreted in different ways. Furthermore, this idea is very uncharacteristic of Judaic tradition; it was, however, widespread in Greco-Roman mythology of that time. We know of many legends of heroes who were born as a result of a peoples' connection with pagan gods—something that is completely absent in Judaism. Actually, the concept of the Holy Spirit as one of the attributes of God was first introduced by the Pharisees, who represented the main movement of Judaism at that time. The Pharisees believed that through the Holy Spirit, the Lord could communicate with humanity and could direct and even possess human beings. Thus, the Messiah—"God's Anointed," the Savior whom the Jewish people awaited—had to be, according to the Pharisees, the bearer of the Holy Spirit, or at least be directed by it. Jesus's disciples, like all the first Christians, believed that Jesus had in himself the Holy Spirit and that his resurrection served as the best proof that he was indeed the true Messiah. Judging by his epistles, it seems that the apostle Paul thought likewise. But the idea of conception by the Holy Spirit was foreign to all movements of Judaism, including the Pharisees. It was not only Jesus's disciples but all of the first Christians as well, including the apostle Paul, who did not see any need in it. If Jesus was the bearer of the Holy Spirit, then did it matter how he was conceived? After all, Jesus was the Son of Man, as he repeatedly reminded his followers. It is likely that in the first 30–40 years of its existence, Christian doctrine did not include at all the idea of Jesus's conception by the Holy Spirit. The letters of Paul (50s CE) and Gospel of Mark (66–69 CE), which are considered the earliest New Testament writings, confirm this. The first appearance of the idea of Immaculate Conception appears in later New Testament books—the gospels of Matthew and Luke (70–80 CE), at a time when many former pagans became members of Christian communities. This idea was brought by the Greeks and Romans; derived from their own pagan cults, it was very familiar and clear to them and helped them better understand the concept of the Jewish Messiah who was to be the bearer of the Holy Spirit. Thus, "the Anointed One," who was called, according to Judaic tradition, to save the Jewish people from Roman oppression, became the Savior—"Christ"—of all humanity, including the Romans. By this time, all of Jesus's disciples and his mother Mary had passed away, which was why the idea of the Immaculate Conception could spread unhindered. However, the fact that the Gospel of John (approximately 100 CE)—the latest of the four gospels—is completely silent on this matter serves as proof that even at the end of the first and beginning of the second centuries CE, this idea had not taken root among Christians and aroused objections from many of them.

The Nativity by Lorenzo Costa. 1490.

The new idea of the circumstances of Christ's birth had its advantages and disadvantages. On the one hand, it helped get rid of the problem of original sin and strengthen the godly status of Jesus; on the other, it gave an excuse for malicious critics of Christianity to doubt the legitimate nature of Jesus's birth. For instance, the Roman pagan writer

Celsus, known for his hostile critique of Christianity, claimed that Mary gave birth to Jesus from a Roman legionnaire before her marriage to Joseph. But Celsus was one of many such opponents of Christianity who exploited the idea of the Immaculate Conception in a dishonest manner.

So while the Bethlehem version was intended to convince the Jews that Jesus fit all the criteria necessary for him to be the Jewish Messiah, the concept of the Immaculate Conception assured the Gentiles of Christ's special, divine status and acquainted them with the Pharisees' perceptions of the Holy Spirit. Both these ideas should be viewed as historical "costs" in the fight for the spread of faith in Jesus. Later, when Christianity had grown stronger and become the state religion, the need for them disappeared; however, by that point, they were part of Christian doctrine, which it would have been unwise to change. Many biblical scholars, particularly Marcus Borg and John Dominic Crossan, are convinced that the stories of Christmas (by Matthew and Luke) are based more on the biblical tradition of the Messiah than on real historical facts (Marcus Borg, John Dominic Crossan, *The First Christmas*, San Francisco: HarperOne, 2009).

When was Jesus born?

This question is not as simple as many think. Today, the overwhelming majority of historians and biblical scholars are convinced that the chronology of the Common Era is set incorrectly due to an error that was made in determining the date of Jesus's birth. This fact is already taken into account by many churches. Even Pope Benedict XVI, in his trilogy *Jesus of Nazareth*, admitted that the Christian calendar is founded on a mistake made by the Roman abbot Dionysius Exiguus (Dionysius the Humble). Benedict believes that, in reality, Jesus was born several years earlier. In 525 CE, Dionysius, on behalf of Pope John I, was composing the so-called Easter tables in order to know when to celebrate Easter. It was then that the Roman monk, who was originally from the Balkan Peninsula, recommended that the Church abandon the old system of year-counting, which began with the first year of the Roman Emperor Diocletian's rule. Diocletian became infamous for his brutal persecution of Christians; using a calendar based on his reign was therefore unacceptable to the Church. So Dionysius suggested a new system of year-counting—one that would begin with the year of Jesus's birth. This he determined through the following deductive method: he first established the alleged date of the crucifixion and then subtracted Jesus's hypothetical age to get the latter's much debatable date of birth. Today, historians and biblical scholars alike consider this calculation method and its result to be unconvincing. But correcting it is not easy. Only the Gospel of Matthew gives information that could help approximate the year of Jesus's birth. According to Matthew, Jesus was born not long before the death of King Herod the Great. But what exactly is meant by "not long before"? The gospel concludes that it is a matter of several months to two years. Before his death, Herod, frightened by prophecies of the Messiah's birth—of the one who was to end his rule—ordered the killing of "all the boys in Bethlehem and its vicinity who were two years old and under, in accordance with the time he had learned from the Magi" (Matthew 2:16). Today, unlike the mistaken Dionysius, we know that Herod died not in the first year of the Common Era (1 CE), but in the fourth year before the Common Era (4 BCE); therefore, based on the Gospel of Matthew, we can conclude that Jesus was born between 6 and 4 BCE. At present, the majority of biblical scholars believe that 4 BCE, the year of Herod's death, seems the more likely date.

However, even here there are difficulties: According to the Jewish historian Flavius Josephus, a lunar eclipse occurred in Judea before the death of Herod. Astronomers confirm that there indeed was a lunar eclipse in 4 BCE in Judea; however, it was likely partial and hardly impressed the people of that time. But they also state that there occurred in Judea a complete lunar eclipse in 1 BCE. So which eclipse was Josephus referring to? What further intensifies the problem is the fact that all our assumptions are based solely on the Gospel of Matthew; after all, Matthew was the only one of the evangelists who deliberately identified Jesus as the new Moses. It was not by chance that he portrayed King Herod as the second Egyptian pharaoh, who ordered the killing of all Jewish newborn boys. Did all this even take place? Why is it that the other three canonical gospels are completely silent on the matter of Herod's glaring crimes? It is unlikely that their authors did not know of such a horrible, merciless massacre directed at Christ. Yet they remain quiet. Thus, associating the year of Jesus's birth with either Herod's persecutions or his death is problematic. The fact that even the Synoptic Gospels of Luke and Mark in no way confirm this connection further strengthens the suspicion that Matthew became too distracted with drawing parallels between Jesus and Moses, as well as between Herod and the Egyptian pharaoh. Unfortunately, even knowing of the inaccuracy committed by the Roman monk Dionysius does not resolve the issue.

Judean Kingdom in the time of Herod the Great (37-4 BCE)

While the year of Jesus's birth can be calculated at least approximately, the month and day are impossible to determine. Placing it at Christmas—now celebrated on the 25th of December (the 7th of January in the Orthodox Church)—is purely symbolic and is in no way associated with Jesus's true date of birth. In the first centuries of the Common Era, Christians did not know of this holiday at all. It was only in the middle of the fourth century of the Common Era that Pope Julius I introduced Christmas as a new holiday and decided it would be celebrated on December 25th. The choice of date was by no means accidental: at this same time, the Romans celebrated the Birthday of the Invincible Sun. Not only the Romans but many pagan peoples celebrated the start of increasing daylight during this period of the year. To distract newly converted Christians from the celebration of the pagan cult, the Roman pope established Christmas, though even then, none of the Church fathers knew Jesus's true date of birth. Thus, a Roman pagan holiday turned into the Christmas we know today.

The many attempts to determine on the basis of the Gospels of Matthew and Luke at least the month or approximate time of the year of Jesus's birth look unconvincing. For instance, the well-known hypothesis that if the shepherds with their cattle stayed in the field during the night Jesus was born, then winter cannot be the time of Christ's birth does not hold up to criticism. The climate of Palestine—and history confirms this—allows grazing cattle even in the winter months. What does not help either is the mention of the bright Star of Bethlehem (according to the Gospel of Matthew), as this phenomenon is interpreted differently by astronomers. All that can safely be said by modern historical science and biblical study is that Jesus was born a few years before the start of the Common Era—nothing more. The majority of churches already agree with this.

Jesus's childhood and youth

This is the only period in Jesus's life that is practically unknown. The canonical gospels say nothing of his childhood and youth. Their silence causes even more doubt with regard to certain details of Jesus's birth described by Matthew and Luke. Information about this period of Jesus's life can be found only in the apocryphal books, such as the Infancy Gospel (of Thomas) and the Syriac Infancy Gospel. But these works are nothing more than fictional stories invented by Gentiles who lived centuries after the crucifixion and had no idea about life in Judea during Jesus's time. The gospel of Luke does mention one episode—namely, what was imprinted in the memory of Mary, Jesus's mother. Luke probably got this information from unpreserved manuscripts written by Jesus's closest followers. Unlike Matthew's fictitious story of the murder of the infants by Herod, we have every reason to believe that this part of Luke's narrative is genuinely an episode from Jesus's childhood. Thus, it is worthwhile to recount it fully:

> Every year Jesus's parents went to Jerusalem for the Festival of
> the Passover. When he was twelve years old, they went up to the

festival, according to the custom. After the festival was over, while his parents were returning home, the boy Jesus stayed behind in Jerusalem, but they were unaware of it. Thinking he was in their company, they traveled on for a day. Then they began looking for him among their relatives and friends. When they did not find him, they went back to Jerusalem to look for him. After three days, they found him in the temple courts, sitting among the teachers, listening to them and asking them questions. Everyone who heard him was amazed at his understanding and his answers. When his parents saw him, they were astonished. His mother said to him, "Son, why have you treated us like this? Your father and I have been anxiously searching for you." "Why were you searching for me?" he asked. "Didn't you know I had to be in my Father's house?" But they did not understand what he was saying to them. Then he went down to Nazareth with them and was obedient to them. But his mother treasured all these things in her heart. And Jesus grew in wisdom and stature, and in favor with God and man. (Luke 2:41–52).

This story testifies not only to the incredible giftedness of the young Jesus but to his thirst for knowledge of the Torah (Pentateuch) and scripture in general. However, in the Galilee of that time, especially in a provincial town like Nazareth, satisfying such a passionate pursuit of learning was not possible. All the most well-known and authoritative experts of the Torah and Judaic tradition lived in Jerusalem; therefore, young men who wanted to study the Tanakh (the Hebrew Bible) flocked to the capital of Judea. But in order to live and study in Jerusalem, both money and time were needed. And although in Jewish tradition, payment was not taken or required to learn Torah, housing and food were not cheap; furthermore, not every family could afford to lose a potential breadwinner to a life of study. It is not hard to conclude from the gospel texts that Jesus's family was big and poor, with relatively low social status. Joseph, the head of the family, was a carpenter by profession, and Jesus had four younger brothers—James, Joseph, Simeon, and Judas—as well as several younger sisters, whose names are not mentioned in the gospels (Matthew 13:55–56). Unlike the apostle Paul, Jesus did not have the means to study and learn from renowned teachers of the law in Jerusalem; otherwise, the gospel authors would have made sure to inform us of it. After all, Paul proudly recalled how he learned the wisdom of the Torah from the famous

Gamaliel I. Jesus, as the eldest son, was forced to remain in Nazareth and help his family until his brothers and sisters grew up. Therefore, he read and learned everything himself, and his success in this regard was proven by extensive scriptural knowledge, which he showed during his preaching and arguments with the Pharisees.

Relationship with John the Baptist

John the Baptist—or Yochanan ha-Mashbil, as his true name sounded in Hebrew—significantly influenced young Jesus's worldview. John did not consider himself a prophet or the new incarnation of Elijah; nor did he view himself as the Messiah (John 1:20–23). He repeated the words of the prophet Isaiah, referring to himself as "the voice of one calling in the wilderness"—a kind of lesson in peoples' conscience; he saw his calling as motivating people to live a righteous way of life. The Gospel of John calls him "a man sent from God. He came as a witness to testify concerning that light, so that through him all might believe. He himself was not the light; he came only as a witness to the light" (John 1:6–8). John the Baptist was a convinced apocalyptic: he awaited the imminent arrival of the Messiah, his judgment of humanity, and the end of the earthly world. John found that the only path to salvation was through repentance and cleansing from sin, and he received his name—"the Baptist" from performing the washing rite, with which he cleansed from sin those who repented. Immersion in water—as a form of purification from sin after one's repentance—was in fact an ancient Judean custom. John had "clothes made of camel's hair, and he had a leather belt around his waist. His food was locusts and wild honey. People went out to him from Jerusalem and all Judea and the whole region of the Jordan. Confessing their sins, they were baptized by him in the Jordan River" (Matthew 3:4–6). Later, this ritual passed into Christianity as one of the elements of baptism. However, while John still baptized with water, the apostles baptized with the Holy Spirit: "For John baptized with water . . . John's baptism was a baptism of repentance. But the apostles baptized with the Holy Spirit" (Acts 1:5; 19:4–6).

John considered himself a forerunner, a precursor of the Messiah, "and this was his message: 'After me comes the one more powerful than I, the straps of whose sandals I am not worthy to stoop down and untie'" (Mark 1:7). Jesus also spoke of John's mission, recalling the words of the prophet Isaiah: "I will send my messenger ahead of you, who will prepare your way before you" (Matthew 11:10–11). Jesus then added: "Truly I tell you, among those born of women there has not risen anyone greater than John the Baptist; yet whoever is least in the kingdom of heaven is greater than he" (Luke 7:27–28). Jesus viewed John as the second incarnation of the prophet Elijah and claimed that "he is the Elijah who was to come" (Matthew 11:14). The mention of Elijah here is not by chance, as according to Judaic tradition, Elijah—the only one of the biblical prophets who was taken into the heavens while still living—was to return before the Messiah's arrival.

John the Baptist was very popular and favored among the Jewish people; in fact, he was much more well-known than Jesus. Notably, Herod Antipas, upon hearing of Jesus, thought about John before all else and said: "John the Baptist has been raised from the dead, and that is why miraculous powers are at work in him" (Mark 6:14). What's more, Josephus mentions John as one of the most respected preachers in Judea, who had great influence on the people. Unlike the gospel version, Josephus explains John's execution not as a consequence of the intrigues of Herod Antipas' wife but as a result of the fear of the ruler himself before the overly influential preacher (*Antiquities of the Jews* 18.5.2). Objectively, John was in a more advantageous position than Jesus. First of all, he preached in Judea itself, not far from Jerusalem and other heavily populated regions of the country, while Jesus's preached mainly to those in less cultured, provincial Galilee. Second, John was of the Aaronites—the highest caste of priesthood—while Jesus mostly likely had no relation to the Aaronites or Levites. And though the gospel of Luke maintains that Mary and Elizabeth—the mothers of Jesus and John, respectively—were relatives, it is likely that the author was driven by the desire to connect Jesus to the family line of the Aaronites and John the Baptist. Here Luke aimed to accomplish two goals: he wanted to give Jesus as much authority in the eyes of Judean aristocrats and priests as possible, and at the same time associate him with the most popular Judean preacher of the time. However, the other canonical gospels do not support this notion.

All the gospels mention Jesus and John together solely in connection with the former's baptism. But did the Messiah need repentance and cleansing from nonexistent sins? Moreover, John baptized him with just water, not with the Holy Spirit. Is this episode an obligatory acknowledgment that Jesus and John not only knew each other well but were also—for a certain period—disciple and teacher, respectively? The canonical gospels were being created 40–70 years after the crucifixion of Christ, when people still had a living memory of the close relations between John and Jesus—as between a teacher and his disciple; therefore, keeping silent on the matter was not an option. Yet the gospel authors feared that direct recognition of this relationship, if it were misinterpreted, would lower Jesus' status among the early Christians: After all, the Messiah could not have been someone's disciple; he himself was the teacher for everyone. So they found an original solution: Jesus was baptized by John and thus, for some time, recognized the latter's authority over himself. In this way, the truth is told—though not in its entirety. Today, those considerations that guided the first evangelists at the dawn of Christianity have lost their relevance, and the fact that Jesus was first a disciple of John the Baptist did not diminish his significance. Contact with John is regarded as a necessary and valuable part of Jesus's earthly life, schooling that prepared him for his own preaching among the Jewish people.

The teacher's influence did not pass without a trace. This is seen in the leitmotif of John's and Jesus's preachings. "Repent, for the kingdom of heaven has come near," John called upon his followers (Matthew 3:2). Jesus similarly called for repentance, stating that the kingdom of God was coming. Many similarities can be found in their preachings, though Jesus was immeasurably more powerful spiritually than his famous teacher. In common were several disciples too. Two followers of John the Baptist (one of them being the apostle Andrew, brother of Peter) joined Jesus (John 1:37–40). In reality, there were more such disciples than are mentioned by the gospels. After John's arrest, practically all his disciples from Galilee went to Jesus, not only Andrew but also Peter, James, and John (the sons of Zebedee), Philip, and Nathaniel. And Jesus's preaching itself, according to the Synoptic gospels, began only after John the Baptist was thrown into prison under the order of Herod Antipas. John himself had chosen Jesus out of all his disciples and blessed him for his preaching. However, if the Gospel of John is to be believed, Jesus began to preach and had his own followers before the imprisonment of John the Baptist (John 3:22–24).

John suspected Jesus' special purpose but was not, to the end of his life, confident that he was indeed the Messiah the Jewish people awaited. The Gospel of Matthew unequivocally mentions this: "When John, who was in prison, heard about the deeds of the Messiah, he sent his disciples to ask him, 'Are you the one who is to come, or should we expect someone else?'" (Matthew 11:2–3). This contradicts the gospels' assertion that John had already been convinced, at the time of Jesus's baptism, that he was the true Messiah. But if John was not yet certain, he was in good company: Even Jesus's disciples fully believed in him as the Messiah only after his resurrection.

Christ Pantocrator. One of the earliest paintings of Jesus.
6th century. Monastery of St Catherine on Mount Sinai.

Unlike John the Baptist, Jesus did not give much importance to fasting and the ascetic way of life. This drew the attention of John's followers. The Gospel of Matthew relates the following: "Then John's disciples came and asked him, 'How is it that we and the Pharisees fast often, but your disciples do not fast?' and Jesus answered, 'How can the guests of the bridegroom mourn while he is with them? The time will come when the bridegroom will be taken from them; then they will fast'" (Matthew 9:14–15). Jesus acknowledged that he looked at fasting and asceticism differently than John. "For John came neither eating nor drinking, and they say, 'He has a demon.' The Son of Man came eating and drinking, and they say, 'Here is a glutton and a drunkard, a friend of tax collectors and sinners'" (Matthew 11:18–19). Thus, he made it clear that the righteous way of life is not necessarily associated with fasting and self-deprivation.

The strong influence of the Essenes is noticeable in both John's and Jesus's preachings, even though New Testament writings say nothing of any connections either had with this religious group. Did the young John, and perhaps Jesus himself, study in the Essene commune? After all, in order to communicate with them, it was not necessary to live in Qumran, in the region of the Judean desert. The Essenes, Josephus states, "have no one certain city, but many of them dwell in every city" (*War of the Jews* 2.8.4). Moreover, according to Josephus, these people willingly accept others' children at the age when they are still receptive to teaching; the Essenes treat these children as if they were their own and teach them their ways (*War of the Jews* 2.8.4). It cannot be excluded that John and Jesus spent their adolescent years among the Essenes, and although they eventually left them, they learned many of their ideas and customs. But there is another possibility as well: that only John lived with the Essenes, and much of what he learned from them he passed on to Jesus as his disciple and apparent successor. In any event, succession: Christ's earthly path lasted only a little longer than John the Baptist's; Jesus was crucified soon after John's execution.

The fate of John the Baptist's followers is quite interesting. Some of them, especially those who were from Galilee, went to Jesus and, after his crucifixion, joined the first Christians; some returned to the Pharisees, who made up the main movement of Judaism at the time; and others united with Judeo-Christian and Gnostic sects—the Ebionites, Hemerobaptists, Elkasaites, and Mandaeans.

The message of Jesus

Jesus repeatedly emphasized that he came to reveal to people the truth about the existence of the Creator's world and what it wants from human beings. He said that humanity is connected to this other, nonmaterial world through the soul—the immortal part of us that was given by God. Jesus considered his primary goal to be the salvation of souls. "For even the Son of Man did not come to be served," he stated, "but to serve, and to give his life as a ransom for many" (Mark 10:45). Clarifying the goal of his mission, he said: "For I did not come to judge the world, but to save the world" (John 12:47). But saving souls could be done only through their repentance, for which many were not ready. The ability to deeply and sincerely repent and have strong faith in God were the criteria that divided the righteous, whose souls would deserve the higher world (the kingdom of God), from the sinners, whose souls could end up in more terrible realms (Gehenna). Speaking of the necessity of separating the true believers from the hypocrites, Jesus warned: "Do you think I came to bring peace on earth? No, I tell you, but division . . . For I have come to turn a man against his father, a daughter against her mother . . . For the Son of Man came to seek and to save the lost" (Luke 12:51; 19:10; Matthew 10:35).

But who did Christ come to save? To this question, Jesus gave an unequivocal and very complete answer: "I have not come to call the righteous, but the sinners" (Mark 2:17). Did he mean all the sinners of our world? Jesus again answers clearly: "I was sent only to the lost sheep of Israel" (Matthew 15:24). Indeed, Christ compared his brethren, the Jews, to children and pagans to dogs. The context for so harsh a statement is that, in those times, the Jewish people, who professed monotheism, regarded themselves as the light of true faith surrounded by paganism and idolatry. At the same time, Jesus admitted that salvation awaits even non-Jews, should they possess a deep and sincere faith in God. Later, in the second century, when the Gentiles began to make up the absolute majority in Christian communities, the copyists added the following phrase in the Gospel of John: "I have other sheep that are not of this sheep pen. I must bring them also. They too will listen to my voice, and there shall be one flock and one shepherd" (John 10:16).

The entire mission of Jesus was accompanied by miracles that had an exclusively positive character. Jesus cured the terminally ill, brought the dead to life, saved the dying, and fed the hungry. He did not punish or ruin anyone, even those who persecuted him and attempted to kill him, despite the fact that the spiritual power he possessed could easily destroy any of his enemies and opponents. It is no coincidence that the gospels mention the fig tree that dried up after Jesus cursed it. This is the only use of Christ's supernatural abilities that was destructive. And it was given with a purpose. The evangelists wanted to emphasize that Jesus not only had power over everyone and everything but could also employ it however he wished. Outside of this instance, he never used it for destructive purposes, even to save his own life. Why? Because the moral he preached excluded any violence. It was because of this that Jesus did not correspond to the traditional portrayals of the Messiah, who was to restore the kingdom of David through military victories. Jesus did not become the peoples' hero and their commander-king. Before him lay a much more important task: become the spiritual Savior and shepherd of the people of Israel. This was the original purpose of Jesus's entire mission. He gave his earthly life not for the redemption of the abstract sins of humanity but for the annunciation of the higher world and to preach about the path to salvation from our material world. Jesus could not allow himself to achieve freedom by using his supernatural powers for destructive purposes. This was clear from the beginning, even during the period of his wanderings with his disciples. For example, when Jews traveled to Jerusalem, the Samaritans did not take them in or offer them rest in their homes; angry, Jesus's closest disciples, James and John, wanted to punish them, but Jesus forbade it, saying that the Son of Man came not to bring ruin to man's souls, but to save them (Luke 9:53–56). Thus, he once again excluded any use of his power for negative purposes. "I have come that they may have life, and have it to the full," he said. "I am the good shepherd. The good shepherd lays down his life for the sheep" (John 10:10–11).

According to the Gospel of Luke, Jesus preached for a fairly short time—only two or three years—beginning at around age thirty. The main themes of his message can be summarized simply: The material world is only a temporary and secondary home for us. Our primary dwelling place is the other, immaterial world of our Creator. Jesus called this other world the "kingdom of God" and the "kingdom of heaven." Human beings should strive not for prosperity and success in our earthly world but for admittance to our Creator's world. But very few truly righteous people are honored with the kingdom of God. The path to this kingdom lies through repentance and acceptance of the new morality, which comprises unconditional love for others, including one's enemies. It is diametrically different from the morality of the Old Testament—"eye for eye, tooth for tooth"—and it is not by chance that this new set of principles has still not taken root in our world.

Jesus taught that predetermination rules the material world; therefore, any attempts of human beings to arrange earthly life in their own way are doomed to fail from the start. On the basis of predestination, Jesus called for nonresistance to evil and obedience to the authorities, as people do not achieve anything through opposition and only cause irreparable damage to their soul. The soul—a special nonmaterial substance that gives life to the body—presents itself as the most important aspect of a human being; the body is earthly dust and is merely a means for improving and perfecting the soul. In the other, immaterial world, the souls will not be divided between men and women, parents and children, husbands and wives. Our material world is a world of suffering, pain, and temptation, existing only for the improvement of our souls.

The real master of our earthly world is a certain "prince" who rules not according to the morals of the kingdom of God but by the laws of matter. Power over us (so that our souls may be tempted) is given to him by the Creator himself, but that power is temporary and limited. Our earthly home, which is, in its way, a purgatory of souls, inevitably will come to an end, but no one, other than God, knows the time of it. Therefore, the people, so as not to damage what's most valuable—their immortal souls, should always be ready for the apocalypse and must care not for multiplying wealth but for leading a righteous way of life.

Jesus considered himself to be the Son of Man, playing the role of mediator between the people and the kingdom of God. It is no coincidence that he was called to be among the Jewish people, as they were the only monotheists of that time and thus most prepared for understanding the morality of our Creator's world. Admittedly, Jesus warned his disciples and followers that he was not the Messiah from whom the people expected victories over the enemies of Israel and the restoration of the kingdom of David. He came for another reason, he said: to call upon the people to repent and, in this way, save their souls. "Unless you repent, you will all perish"—in this reminder and warning was the essence of Jesus's message (Luke 13:3,5).

Jesus's preaching in the light of Judaism's laws

In Christian literature, there formed a viewpoint that Jesus's preaching principally differed from the ideas and practice of Judaism of that time. In reality, the texts of the canonical gospels do not confirm this. Moreover, the gospel texts testify that Jesus firmly stood on the ground of Judaism's laws, carrying them out not formally, as his critics did, but essentially. It should not be forgotten that Judaism at the time of Jesus was not one monolithic teaching but several relatively different religious directions. In some instances, Jesus's preaching converged with and was in fact identical to the views of the Pharisees; in others, it had much in common with the Essenes. Jesus did not revoke the laws of Judaism but taught that they should be honestly and sincerely adhered to. This is best shown by the gospel texts: "Do not think that I have come to abolish the Law or the Prophets"—said Jesus—"I have not come to abolish them but to fulfill them" (Matthew 5:17). Jesus also acknowledged the authority of the Sanhedrin—the supreme Judean court. The fact that Christ was ready to turn over to the court "anyone who is angry with his brother" attests to his respect toward this supreme religious and judicial authority (Matthew 5:22). Thus, any attempt to separate Jesus from Judaism is unsubstantiated. Much more interesting is another issue—what Jesus brought to Judaism and how he interpreted Moses's laws.

The texts of the canonical gospels delineate three tendencies in Jesus's approach to the laws of Judaism. The first of these tendencies manifested itself in much stricter demands to adhere to several key rules of the Written Torah (Pentateuch). The following are only a few examples of Jesus' sterner view of the fulfillment of the Mosaic laws: "You have heard"—he said—"that it was said to the people long ago, 'You shall not murder, and anyone who murders will be subject to judgment.' But I tell you that anyone who is angry with his brother will be subject to judgment. Again, anyone who says to his brother 'Raca' [fool] is answerable to the court. And anyone who says, 'You fool!' will be in danger of the fire of hell" (Matthew 5:21–22).

Jesus was equally intransigent to adultery: "You have heard that it was said, 'You shall not commit adultery.' But I tell you that anyone who looks at a woman lustfully has already committed adultery with her in his heart. If your right eye causes you to stumble, gouge it out and throw it away. It is better for you to lose one part of your body than for your whole body to be thrown into hell" (Matthew 5:27–29).

Divorce was a matter that Jesus treated more strictly than Moses: "It has been said, 'Anyone who divorces his wife must give her a certificate of divorce.' But I tell you that anyone who divorces his wife, except for sexual immorality, makes her the victim of adultery, and anyone who marries a divorced woman commits adultery" (Matthew 5:31–32). Jesus was convinced, "what God has joined together, let no one separate" (Matthew 19:6). He saw only one reason for divorce—adultery, and when the Pharisees reminded him that the lawgiver, Moses himself, permitted divorce, Jesus countered with the following: "Moses permitted you to divorce your wives because your hearts were hard. But it was not this way from the beginning" (Matthew 19:8). Jesus's approach to divorce was so strict that even his disciples could not but notice: "If this is the situation between a husband and wife, it is better not to marry." But Jesus gave them a noteworthy answer: "Not everyone can accept this word, but only those to whom it has been given" (Matthew 19:10–11).

Jesus held the same uncompromising position regarding all oaths:

> Again, you have heard that it was said to the people long ago, "Do not break your oath, but fulfill to the Lord the vows you have made." But I tell you, do not swear an oath at all: either by heaven, for it is God's throne; or by the earth, for it is his footstool; or by Jerusalem, for it is the city of the Great King. And do not swear by your head, for you cannot make even one hair white or black. All you need to say is simply "Yes" or "No"; anything beyond this comes from the evil one. (Matthew 5:33–37).

The second tendency is associated with Jesus's attitude to the laws of the so-called Oral Torah, which were later recorded in the Mishnah, then in the Talmud, and finally, in the twelfth century, in the Halakha. Unlike the rules of the Written Torah (Pentateuch), Moses never recorded them anywhere; however, the Pharisees claimed that the lawgiver passed them on to the Levites in oral form. It remains unclear why Moses deemed it necessary to record one set of laws but not the other. The priests of Jerusalem's Temple, representing another direction in Judaism—the Sadducees—did not recognize the Oral Torah and considered it to be the creation of the Pharisees themselves. Contrary to the Sadducees, Jesus accepted the laws of the Oral Torah, but unlike the Pharisees, believed they came from the people, not God, and thus treated them fairly liberally. In particular, he approached the laws of Sabbath observance very flexibly, asserting that man was not created for the Sabbath but the Sabbath for man (Mark 2:27). The gospels give many examples of this. "At that time,

Jesus went through the grainfields on the Sabbath. His disciples were hungry and began to pick some heads of grain and eat them. When the Pharisees saw this, they said to him, 'Look! Your disciples are doing what is unlawful on the Sabbath.' He answered, 'Haven't you read what David did when he and his companions were hungry? He entered the house of God, and he and his companions ate the consecrated bread—which was not lawful for them to do, but only for the priests'" (Matthew 12:1–4). Jesus's opinion is better expressed in the episode in which a sick man is healed on the Sabbath, in the synagogue:

> He went into their synagogue, and a man with a shriveled hand was there. Looking for a reason to bring charges against Jesus, they asked him, "Is it lawful to heal on the Sabbath?" He said to them, "If any of you has a sheep and it falls into a pit on the Sabbath, will you not take hold of it and lift it out? How much more valuable is a person than a sheep! Therefore it is lawful to do good on the Sabbath." Then he said to the man, "Stretch out your hand." So he stretched it out and it was completely restored, just as sound as the other. (Matthew 12:9–13).

The Gospel of John mentions another statement of Jesus on this occasion: "Now if a boy can be circumcised on the Sabbath so that the Law of Moses may not be broken, why are you angry with me for healing a man's whole body on the Sabbath?" (John 7:23).

The question of what to do during Sabbath—on the day of rest and prayer—was really important for the Jews. In their reverence for the Sabbath, the *Hasideans* (pious), who were the Pharisees' ideological predecessors, went to the point of allowing their enemies to kill them during the Maccabean wars, fearing that any opposition might desecrate the sacred day. Jesus separated the laws of Judaism into those given by God and those added by man. While he demanded that the former be strictly followed, he taught that the latter should be adhered to only when possible and without losing common sense.

Finally, another difference in Jesus's approach to the laws of Judaism was the preaching of a completely new morality, sharply different from that of the Old Testament. Rooted in neither the Written nor the Oral Torah, this morality was rather a reflection of the world of our Creator. Addressing the people with the Sermon on the Mount, Jesus said:

You have heard that it was said, "Eye for eye, and tooth for tooth."
But I tell you, do not resist an evil person. If anyone slaps you on the
right cheek, turn to them the other cheek also. And if anyone wants
to sue you and take your shirt, hand over your coat as well. If anyone
forces you to go one mile, go with them two miles. Give to the one
who asks you, and do not turn away from the one who wants to bor-
row from you. (Matthew 5:38–42)

From this principle logically flowed another:

You have heard that it was said, "Love your neighbor and hate your
enemy." But I tell you, love your enemies and pray for those who
persecute you, that you may be children of your Father in heaven.
He causes his sun to rise on the evil and the good, and sends rain
on the righteous and the unrighteous. If you love those who love
you, what reward will you get? Are not even the tax collectors doing
that? . . . Be perfect, therefore, as your heavenly Father is perfect.
(Matthew 5:43–46,48)

Jesus put special emphasis on forgiveness. His answer to Peter, his closest disciple, is very characteristic of this. When the latter asked, "Lord,
how many times shall I forgive my brother when he sins against me? Up
to seven times?" Jesus answered, "I tell you, not seven times, but seventy-
seven times" (Matthew 18:21–22). The ideas of forgiveness, mercy, unconditional love, and nonresistance to evil were unquestionably a new
trend in Judaism of that time and represented, apart from the Pharisees,
Sadducees, and Essenes, the appearance of another religious direction—
that of the so-called Nazarenes; admittedly, this new direction formed
completely only after the crucifixion of Jesus.

The Kingdom of God

The Judaism of Jesus's time had very vague ideas about the afterlife. The
Pharisees believed that after one's death the soul transitioned to another, immaterial world; they did not know what form it took there. The
Sadducees—priests of the Temple of Jerusalem and direct descendants of
the Aaronites— denied that an afterlife existed. The Old Testament says
almost nothing about the world beyond the boundary of human life—and
probably, not by chance. "You set a boundary they cannot cross," states

one of the biblical psalms, declaring that man will never be able to comprehend the depth of the Lord's intentions (Psalm 104:9). Our Creator initially set some limits for the breadth of man's knowledge, and one can only assume that this was done for the sake of humanity itself.

An episode from the life of the Israelite king Saul sheds some light on early biblical views of the afterworld: On the eve of the fatal battle with the Philistines at Mount Gilboa, Saul summoned the soul of the prophet and judge Samuel, in order to learn about his fate. But so terrible was his answer, it would have been better if he had not asked at all: "Tomorrow you and your sons will be with me" (I Samuel 28:19). And so, in ancient Israel there existed wizards and sorceresses who summoned the souls of the deceased, but—and this is noteworthy—Yahwist priests, pointing to the will of God, not only refused to do this themselves but also categorically forbade others to perform such an act, deeming it paganism and sin. It is no coincidence that Saul had difficulty finding a woman who could call upon the souls of the dead, as he himself, at the insistence of the high priest, had ordered the persecution and extermination of such individuals. Early and late Judaism alike permitted people to communicate only with God—either directly with him or through his intermediaries (such as his prophets). The same injunction passed unchanged to Christianity.

Jesus was the first to bring us some knowledge of the afterworld, and not from pagans and idolaters, but from the kingdom of God. In man, the "dust of the earth," there is only one immortal part—the soul, which, at the end of life, transitions to the immaterial world. But to imagine the soul's stay in this other world as a continuation of earthly life was wrong in Jesus's view. In answer to the Sadducees, who did not believe in either the existence of souls or the afterlife, Jesus said, "When the dead rise, they will neither marry nor be given in marriage; they will be like the angels in heaven" (Mark 12:25). Jesus warned that in the "kingdom of Heaven" or "kingdom of God"—as he called the immaterial world in order to be more easily understood—things are not as they are here. "What people value highly is detestable in God's sight . . . So the last will be first, and the first will be last . . . Truly I tell you, the tax collectors and the prostitutes are entering the kingdom of God ahead of you. For John came to you to show you the way of righteousness, and you did not believe him, but the tax collectors and the prostitutes did. And even after you saw this, you did not repent and believe him" (Luke 16:15; Matthew 20:16; 21:31–32).

Jesus, attempting to reach the level of his listeners (who were simple and unschooled), schematically divided the afterworld into two parts: one gave "eternal life," the other "eternal punishment" (Matthew 25:46). He conveyed the idea of the different fates that awaited the righteous and the sinners in the story of Lazarus and the rich man. The rich man, having received all the good already during his lifetime, suffers in hell after his death, while the righteous Lazarus, who came across only evil in his earthly life, is comforted by "Abraham's side." Between the first and second is "a great chasm that has been set in place," one that cannot be crossed (Luke 16:19–26). This parable speaks of two things at once: first, that reward for one's good deeds and retribution for sins are inevitable, and second, that they usually come only in the other, immaterial world.

"The Lord—God of the living, not the dead"

Speaking of man's connection with the Lord's incorporeal world, Jesus added new input to previous biblical views of the soul. He rethought a very renowned biblical phrase: "The Lord—God of the living, not the dead." The ancients were convinced man's death interrupts his connection with God. The following psalm of King David is very characteristic of this: "Turn, Lord, and deliver me; save me because of your unfailing love. Among the dead, no one proclaims your name. Who praises you from the grave?" (Ps. 6:4–5). Early biblical authors believed that death put an end not only to an individual's relationship with God but to God's power over them, too: "Do you show your wonders to the dead? Do their spirits rise up and praise you? Is your love declared in the grave, your faithfulness in Destruction?" (Ps. 88:10–11). The meaning of these psalms is that the deceased do not know God and cannot praise him, while the Lord is deprived of the opportunity to perform miracles over them. It was because of this belief that the early authors of the Bible asked for their lives to be extended so that they could continue giving praise to God. Jesus changed this phrase, giving it a different meaning: "He is not the God of the dead, but of the living, for to him all are alive" (Luke 20:38). Jesus meant that for God, all are living—even those who had concluded their earthly paths long ago; it is not about the dust of the earth—that is, the physical body—but rather about the soul, which remains in his hands and under his power even after one's death, and which continues its existence in the immaterial world. In this way, Jesus emphasized that for God, the corporeal shell of the soul does not matter at all and that this shell merely constitutes temporary, material "clothing," which can repeatedly change.

Jesus was forced to reckon with the fact that his listeners comprised mostly uneducated, common people of Galilee; therefore, he tried to talk in parables and simplify abstract concepts as much as possible. In spite of this, his statements about souls being in the kingdom of God indicate that over time these immortal, immaterial substances lose the personalities and memories individuals they once had. As a result, the division of human beings into men and women, husbands and wives, parents and children—including all family ties and all other characteristics of our earthly existence—are totally absent in the immaterial world. Souls of relatives whose deaths were many years apart will not be able to recognize each other in the afterworld. However, if they achieved a similar degree of moral perfection on earth, they will be together on the same level in the immaterial world. In attempting to explain all this, Jesus said simply: "My Father's house has many rooms" (John 14:2).

Who rules our world?

The ancients knew that they lived in a world dominated by evil. Times changed, rulers were replaced, but evil remained. The first authors of the Bible talk about this with pain: "Help, Lord, for no one is faithful anymore; those who are loyal have vanished from the human race. Everyone lies to their neighbor; they flatter with their lips but harbor deception in their hearts . . . The wicked, who freely strut about when what is vile is honored by the human race" (Ps. 12:1–2,7–8). People had long wondered and asked: Could our world be from God if there is so much evil and injustice in it? The apostle James (brother of Jesus) wrote sharply: "You adulterous people, don't you know that friendship with the world means enmity against God? Therefore, anyone who chooses to be a friend of the world becomes an enemy of God" (James 4:4). Could this have been said if our world was truly controlled by God?

Another apostle, John, testified that the earthly world is not from God: "Do not love the world or anything in the world. If anyone loves the world, love for the Father is not in them. For everything in the world—the lust of the flesh, the lust of the eyes, and the pride of life—comes not from the Father but from the world" (I John 2:15–16). The apostle divided all people into two unequal parts: the absolute majority, who "are from the world and therefore speak from the viewpoint of the world, and the world listens to them . . ." and the select few who are "from God." But one who is part of this select few is much greater than the one belonging to the majority. "We know—stated John—that we are children of God, and that the whole world is under the control of the evil one" (I John 4:5; 5:19).

Jesus separated himself and his disciples from the surrounding world, as it was incapable of accepting the Spirit of truth. The world cannot accept him "because it neither sees him nor knows him" (John 14:17). On the night before his arrest, Jesus warned his disciples, telling them to be brave: "In this world you will have trouble. But take heart!" (John 16:33). He said that in him they will have peace, and in his prayer to the Father, Jesus unequivocally expressed his attitude to our world: "I am not praying for the world, but for those you have given me, for they are yours . . . They are not of the world, even as I am not of it" (John 17:9,16).

Jesus repeats the same thing to his followers: "If you belonged to the world, it would love you as its own. As it is, you do not belong to the world, but I have chosen you out of the world. That is why the world hates you" (John 15:19). Jesus's openness in opposing himself to our world was noted by his disciples: "Then Judas [not Judas Iscariot] said, 'But, Lord, why do you intend to show yourself to us and not to the world?'" And Jesus replied: "My peace I give you" (John 14:22, 27).

In this way, Jesus makes it clear that the world we live in is not from God and that if we wish to enter his kingdom, we can arrive there only through him. "I am the way and the truth and the life. No one comes to the Father except through me" (John 14:6). But if our material world, brought into existence, like everything, by one Creator, is not controlled by him, then who is its real master, and why was it given to him by God himself?

Jesus gave an answer to the first part of the question the night before his arrest. He told his disciples:

> It is for your good that I am going away. Unless I go away, the Counselor will not come to you; but if I go, I will send him to you. When he comes, he will prove the world to be in the wrong about sin and righteousness and judgment: about sin, because people do not believe in me; about righteousness, because I am going to

the Father, where you can see me no longer; and about judgment because the prince of this world now stands condemned. I have much more to say to you, more than you can now bear. (John 16:7–12)

And so, our material world is controlled by a certain prince, who is already condemned by the Lord. But this is not the only time that Jesus mentions who rules our world. On the eve of the end of his earthly mission, Jesus again addressed his disciples: "I will not say much more to you, for the prince of this world is coming. He has no hold over me" (John 14:30).

If this prince, the ruler of our earthly lives, has nothing in common with Christ, then how can we say that our world is from God? Even if our material world was initially created by the Lord, the issue remains: It is not controlled by him. But why are we given into the power of a certain "prince" whose laws are as different from God's commandments as our earthly world is from the kingdom of God?

Jesus responded to this second part of the question in his preachings, calling upon the people to repent as a means of salvation from the rule of this prince—and the only path to the kingdom of God. Jesus often stated that for God, our bodies—the corporeal shells made of earth's dust—carried no importance; what mattered to him were the special, immaterial substances that we call souls. It is this immortal part that fills the material body with life and leaves it lifeless upon departing. Only this special, spiritual energy is of interest to the Creator, who, with its help, is transforming the universe. Our material world, like our earthly civilization, was created primarily for the improvement of these spiritual substances. By nature, however, our souls can improve only through suffering, torment, and struggle. Conflicts, wars, revolutions, social collisions—all these are a necessary background for personal stress and moral pain, which make possible qualitative development in our souls, an essential requirement put forth by God. Yet not only are people tested with pain and suffering, they are also tempted with power, wealth, and success. The fate of those who failed to resist earthly blessings is not enviable: Their souls are doomed to severe suffering in their new body shells. If souls undergo negative development that leads to moral degradation, they are sent to worlds more terrible than our own—to Gehenna ("Burning Hell"), as Jesus had talked about. Morally perfect souls (the righteous) do not return to our terrible, material world; they remain in Jesus's kingdom of God. But the fate of the absolute majority is to be sent back to our earthly world—the purgatory of souls, whose master is the very prince that Jesus had mentioned. Apparently, the evolution of our souls would not have been possible without this prince and the blatant injustice, meanness, and temptations of his world. This is the purpose of the prince of darkness, and it is for this that he received his power from God. But as Jesus warned, the Lord has already condemned this prince, and so the latter's rule is temporary—till the end of our world. Moreover, his control is limited, as sincere and passionate prayer to God may overrule the prince's will. Notable are the words of the only prayer known to us that Jesus gave to his disciples—the Lord's Prayer. As it says, "Our Father in heaven, hallowed be your name, your kingdom come, your will be done, on earth as it is in heaven" (Matthew 6:9–10). These words acknowledge that God does not rule our material world, which is why we are calling upon him to intervene and spread his own power over it. And again, the same prayer asks: ". . . and lead us not into temptation, but deliver us from the evil one" (Matthew 6:13)—that is, it asks for freedom from the rule of the prince of darkness, who controls us. We appeal to the Lord because it was he who made all the known and unknown (to us) worlds and reigns over this very prince: "For thine is the kingdom, and the power, and the glory, for ever and ever. Amen" (Doxology. Didache 8:2; Episcopal BCP).

Like the material world, people do not live, nor can they live, by the laws of the kingdom of God. Only a select few are able to do so. But according to the apostle Paul, in order to enter the kingdom of God it is necessary to live by the spirit, not the flesh. "Those who are in the realm of the flesh cannot please God" (Romans 8:8).

On nonresistance to evil and authority

If our earthly world—one of suffering and pain—is merely a tool for improving human souls, then both evil and the evil prince's rule are inevitable and necessary. In that case, resisting the rule of the prince and his servants would mean going against the will of God, who created our world as it is. On the other hand, our stay in this earthly world entails being under the laws of the "prince of darkness," who will never allow justice and truth to triumph; thus, there is no sense in fighting for what is, in principle, unattainable in the material world. For by destroying one injustice, we involuntarily create another. Furthermore, any resistance to offenders may lead one to commit no less evil than those very wrong-doers and inflict an irreparable blow to one's soul. Bearing in mind that our material world is ephemeral and transitory, Jesus taught that people should care not about their bodies, which were destined to turn into dust, but about their immortal souls and should avoid everything that could make it difficult to reach the kingdom of God. Any disobedience to earthly authorities, he taught, threatened to result in violence, which could aggravate the fate of one's soul. In this lies the main reason why Jesus rejected any resistance to evil. Instead, he proposed to defeat evil through repentance and love. He spread unconditional love not only to friends and neighbors but to offenders and enemies as well, preaching that only in this way would it be possible to enter the kingdom of God, as well as accelerate the end of the earthly world and the evil prince's power over it.

More difficult to understand is Jesus's attitude to the Romans in Judea. None of the canonical gospels contain any clear remarks of Jesus on this matter. However, there is an episode in which Jesus, tempted by the scribes, speaks unambiguously in favor of payment of taxes. "Give back to Caesar what is Caesar's, and to God what is God's," he states (Luke 20:25). Of course, payment of taxes does not imply blind obedience to Roman authorities. Furthermore, biblical scholars specializing in the study of evangelical texts believe that this episode was an addition made by later editors of the New Testament writings. So the question remains: What was Jesus's attitude to Rome?

Unlike his disciples and the apostles of early Christianity, Jesus tried to avoid expressing his opinion of the Romans. Given the heated political atmosphere in Judea of that time, this would have been unsafe. The Jewish people hated the Roman occupiers and their appointed local authorities. Galilee, the birthplace of Jesus, was the heart of the Jewish resistance; Roman procurators had to call reinforcements from Syria on more than one occasion in order to organize "sweeps" of places native to Jesus. Condemning the authorities was as dangerous as supporting them. In the first case, there was the threat of clashing with the Romans; in the second, with their own people. Judging by the spirit of Jesus's preaching, he could not call for revolt against Rome or disobedience to its appointees. Those historians who assume that Jesus was a failed leader of the Jewish Resistance are greatly mistaken (Hyam Maccoby, *Revolution in Judea: Jesus and the Jewish Resistance*, 1981). In reality, Jesus, who called for turning the other cheek—that very Jesus who urged the people to pray for their offenders and enemies—could not, in any way, enter into conflict with the authorities. In this respect, we can completely trust the words of his closest disciple, the apostle Peter: "Submit yourselves for the Lord's sake to every human authority: whether to the emperor, as the supreme authority, or to governors, who are sent by him to punish those who do wrong and to commend those who do right." Furthermore, Peter excluded any disobedience in principle:

> Slaves, in reverent fear of God submit yourselves to your masters, not only to those who are good and considerate, but also to those who are harsh. For it is commendable if someone bears up under the pain of unjust suffering because they are conscious of God. But how is it to your credit if you receive a beating for doing wrong and endure it? But if you suffer for doing good and you endure it, this is commendable before God. (I Peter 2:13–14, 18–20)

When calling upon the first Christians to submit before the evil of our world, Peter always gave the example of his teacher: "When they hurled their insults at him, he did not retaliate; when he suffered, he made no threats. Instead, he entrusted himself to him who judges justly" (I Peter 2:23).

On the meaning of faith

Jesus gave exceptional importance to one's profound faith, as he believed that without it, people not only would miss entering the kingdom of God, they would not even receive answers to their prayers. "Truly I tell you, if anyone says to this mountain, 'Go, throw yourself into the sea,' and does not doubt in their heart but believes that what they say will happen, it will be done for them. Therefore I tell you, whatever you ask for in prayer, believe that you have received it, and it will be yours" (Mark 11:23–24). But for the people, including his own disciples, it was the sincerity and depth of faith that constituted a serious issue: They doubted everything and could not fully believe. Noteworthy is the confession of a man who brought his son to Jesus in order to cast out the demons in him: "I do believe; help me overcome my unbelief!" he exclaimed with tears in his eyes (Mark 9:24).

The Healing of Blind Bartimaeus. Araldo de Luca/Corbis.

The problem of faith was present even two thousand years ago. In order to believe the words of Jesus, people demanded miracles from him. But having received them in abundance, they continued to doubt. It was not without reason that Jesus taught that faith should be founded not on fear and miracles but on conviction in the truth of what one believes. Referring to incomplete, or even totally insincere faith, Jesus warned: "Truly I tell you, anyone who will not receive the kingdom of God like a little child will never enter it" (Mark 10:15). And only true faith can, according to Jesus's words, save man from disease and injury. For instance, the blind man Bartimaeus, son of Timaeus, from Jericho, firmly believed—unlike his compatriots—that Jesus was the Messiah from the lineage of David and, unafraid of punishment, openly proclaimed this before the people. "'What do you want me to do for you?' Jesus asked him. The blind man said, 'Rabbi, I want to see.' 'Go,' said Jesus, 'your faith has healed you.' Immediately he received his sight and followed Jesus along the road" (Mark 10:51–52).

The best example of unconditional faith in Jesus' strength and power was a foreigner—a Roman centurion from Capernaum who was very sympathetic to the Jewish people. This Roman had a servant he valued highly who was very ill and near death, and he sent word to ask if Jesus would heal him. But when Jesus was near his house, he sent a message saying he was not worthy to receive a visit from him, and asked instead that Jesus simply give the order—just as the centurion did with those under his command—and his servant will be healed. "When

Jesus heard this, he was amazed at him, and turning to the crowd following him, he said, 'I tell you, I have not found such great faith even in Israel'" (Luke 7:9).

From those who wanted to beg for forgiveness from the Lord, Jesus demanded not only faith but also the exact same forgiveness with regard to their debtors and offenders. "For if you forgive other people when they sin against you, your heavenly Father will also forgive you. But if you do not forgive others their sins, your Father will not forgive your sins" (Matthew 6:14–15).

The apostle James, brother of Jesus, later reminded the people of Jesus's warning—that communicating with the Lord without faith is useless. One must always ask with faith—he claimed—"But when you ask, you must believe and not doubt, because the one who doubts is like a wave of the sea, blown and tossed by the wind. That person should not expect to receive anything from the Lord. Such a person is double-minded and unstable in all they do" (James 1:6–8).

Jesus did not condemn those who did not believe in him. He said: "If anyone hears my words but does not keep them, I do not judge that person. For I did not come to judge the world, but to save the world" (John 12:47).

Jesus—an apocalyptic?

The early biblical authors already understood that the earthly world surrounding us was not eternal and, sooner or later, would come to its end. One can only be astonished at the insight and depth of thought of those, who almost three thousand years ago, addressing God, wrote the following words: "In the beginning you laid the foundations of the earth, and the heavens are the work of your hands. They will perish, but you remain; they will all wear out like a garment. Like clothing you will change them and they will be discarded. But you remain the same, and your years will never end" (Ps. 102:25–27).

The thought of the apocalypse—that is, the inevitable end of our material world—arose in the Bible very long ago, long before the appearance of Jesus. But only during the time of Jesus did this idea begin to rapidly spread and become clearly expressed: Many people expected the end of the world and the coming of the Messiah during their lifetime. Those who believed that the end of our earthly world would come very soon were called apocalyptics. Such were John the Baptist, the disciples of Jesus, the apostle Paul, and, generally, all of the first Christians. This is best demonstrated by their own words.

Here is what the apostle James, the brother of Jesus, wrote to the first Christian communities: "You, too, be patient and stand firm, because the Lord's coming is near" (James 5:8). Jesus's closest disciple, the apostle Peter, thought just the same: "The end of all things is near. Therefore be alert and of sober mind so that you may pray" (1 Peter 4:7). A similar idea was expressed by John the Evangelist, author of the gospel and of three canonical letters: "And now, dear children, continue in him, so that when he appears we may be confident and unashamed before him at his coming" (1 John 2:28).

John the Evangelist was the author of another New Testament book, the Book of Revelation, where he similarly showed himself to be a convinced apocalyptic, awaiting the fast-approaching end of the world and second coming of the Messiah. "Then he told me, 'Do not seal up the words of the prophecy of this scroll, because the time is near. Let the one who does wrong continue to do wrong; let the vile person continue to be vile; let the one who does right continue to do right; and let the holy person continue to be holy . . . Look, I am coming soon! My reward is with me, and I will give to each person according to what they have done'" (Rev. 22:10–12). And finally, so that no one doubts the fast-approaching end of the world and Jesus' second coming, John ends his book of prophecies with the following phrase: "He who testifies to these things says, 'Yes, I am coming soon.' Amen. Come, Lord Jesus" (Rev. 22:20).

And so, Christ's circle and all his followers believed in the fast-approaching end of the world and the coming of the Messiah. But what did Jesus think of this? Was he, too, an apocalyptic? The majority of biblical scholars believe that he was, but the texts of the canonical gospels do not allow an unequivocal conclusion. The problem is that the authors of the gospels, writing of Christ 40 to 70 years after his crucifixion, mixed Jesus' statements on two completely different events that were destined to happen.

The first was the prophecy of the impending destruction of the Temple and fall of Judea. Jesus did not indicate when it would happen, but he knew for sure it was to occur during the lifetime of his generation. "Truly I tell you, this generation will certainly not pass away until all these things have happened" (Luke 21:32). And, indeed, the Jewish-Roman War, the destruction of the country, and the banishment of the people from their homeland all occurred around 40 years after the crucifixion of Jesus.

Second was the prediction of the nearing end of the world and the second coming of the Son of Man, who would judge everyone. And in this case, Jesus, in contrast to false prophets, admits that he does not know the exact date of the apocalypse: "But about that day or hour no one knows, not even the angels in heaven, nor the Son, but only the Father . . . Therefore keep watch, because you do not know on what day your Lord will come" (Matthew 24:36,42). By "keeping watch," Jesus meant the righteous way of life, prayer, fasting—everything that makes human beings morally prepared for the apocalypse.

Still, during his life, Jesus tried to separate his predictions of these two completely different events: the destruction of Jerusalem and Judea and the end of the world. "When you hear of wars and uprisings, do not be frightened. These things must happen first, but the end will not come right away" (Luke 21:9). Due to the time it took to traverse long distances and, more importantly, the transfer of information through second, third, and even fourth hands, the words of Christ about significant events were distorted or misunderstood, as were many other episodes from the lives of Jesus and his disciples. Thus suffered not only the accuracy of the sequence of events but also the integrity of Jesus' statements. This incomplete and inaccurate narrative, combined with the confused chronology, was already present in the original texts of the canonical gospels. For instance, the Gospel of Luke, having taken from Mark's gospel Jesus's warning of horrible disasters that would befall Judea (by that was meant the Great Jewish Revolt against Rome), used it as a prophecy about the end of the world (Luke 17:26–29). Still, all this is nothing compared to the distortions added to the gospels by the second-century copyists.

The biblical scholars claiming that Jesus was an apocalyptic always cite the following words of Christ from the Gospel of Luke: "Truly I tell you, some who are standing here will not taste death before they see the kingdom of God" (Luke 9:27). They interpret this statement as indisputable proof that Jesus believed in the impending end of the world, which would occur during the lives of some of his disciples. However, another interpretation of these words is possible—namely, that there are people of such righteousness that their souls will be worthy of the kingdom of God during their earthly lives. Moreover, the immortal soul is the only part of human beings that connects them to God's world and belongs to him, while the souls of the righteous already represent the grains of the kingdom of God. Supporting this interpretation is another of Jesus' statements from the Gospel of Luke: "Once, on being asked by the Pharisees when the kingdom of God would come, Jesus replied, 'The coming of the kingdom of God is not something that can be observed, nor will people say, 'Here it is,' or 'There it is,' because the kingdom of God is in your midst'" (Luke 17:20–21). After this, can Jesus be considered an apocalyptic?

Son of Man

Who did Jesus consider himself to be, and how did he identify himself to the people? Here, all three Synoptic Gospels significantly diverge from the Gospel of John. According to Mark, Luke, and Matthew, Jesus behaved like the Messiah but while performing miracles forbade everyone to talk about them. Why? First of all, to not clash with Roman authorities and their henchmen—the priests of Jerusalem's Temple. The Romans saw in the Messiah's appearance anti-Roman rebellion; after all, the Savior was to drive them out and become king of Judea. The priests viewed any new religious leader as a threat to their authority. This was why Jesus performed his miracles unwillingly. And he was constrained to do so not only because of mercy to the suffering but also on account of the popular conviction that the true Messiah would perform supernatural feats. Without miracles, the people were not ready to believe in Jesus. But any one of these miracles aroused suspicion from the authorities and priests; therefore, Jesus, upon healing the terminally ill, asked them not to say anything of it (Mark 8:22–26). And so, according to the Synoptic Gospels, Jesus knew that he was the Messiah (and so thought his disciples) but, for the time being, deemed it necessary to keep it secret, especially from the authorities (Mark 16:20).

In the Gospel of John, Jesus no longer hides anything from anyone: He widely and publicly proclaims himself the Messiah. But even here is an episode that supports the point of view of the Synoptic Gospels. Thus, in the Temple of Jerusalem, "the Jews who were there gathered around him, saying, 'How long will you keep us in suspense? If you are the Messiah, tell us plainly'" (John 10:24). Consequently, Jesus, in reality, carefully concealed that he considered himself the Messiah, rightly fearing confrontation with Roman authorities. It is likely that Jesus's claims that he is the Messiah and the Son of God came as additions to the texts made by copyists in the second century, when they basically took advantage of their complete freedom to edit the gospels.

At the same time, before Jesus was another problem: In his native Nazareth, the people saw him as a regular man, neither the Messiah nor even a prophet. It was his compatriots and those who knew his family who showed the most skepticism:

> "Isn't this the carpenter? Isn't this Mary's son and the brother of James, Joseph, Judas, and Simeon? Aren't his sisters here with us?" And they took offense at him. Jesus said to them, "A prophet is not without honor except in his own town, among his relatives and in his own home." He could not do any miracles there except lay his hands on a few sick people and heal them. He was amazed at their lack of faith. (Mark 6:3–6)

Any mention of his mother, brothers, and sisters emphasized his purely human nature and essentially belittled him in the eyes of the people. In response, Jesus avoiding calling himself the Messiah and tried to appear before the people not as a member of his family but as a spokesman of God's will. In this respect, very typical is the following episode from the Gospel of Mark:

> Then Jesus's mother and brothers arrived. Standing outside, they sent someone in to call him. A crowd was sitting around him, and they told him, "Your mother and brothers are outside looking for you." "Who are my mother and my brothers?" he asked. Then he looked at those seated in a circle around him and said, "Here are my mother and my brothers! Whoever does God's will is my brother and sister and mother." (Mark 3:31–35).

If Jesus was unwilling to publicly admit that he was the Messiah but also did not want to be perceived as a regular man, who did he present himself to be to the Jewish people? Jesus called himself the Son of Man. This name came from the Old Testament and meant no more than belongingness to the human race. It was used the same way by the prophet Ezekiel. It was only the prophet Daniel who gave an entirely new meaning to this name. According to the book of his prophecies, God will give eternal rule over the world to the "Son of Man" (Daniel 7:13–14). The prediction implied that the Son of Man must come from among the Jewish people and become the mediator between the people and God; however, it did not determine the nature of this Son. Later, as the idea of the Savior spread, the name Son of Man was perceived as one of the definitions of this Messiah. But these names were not identical to each other. While the Messiah had to be the

Son of Man, the latter did not have to be the Savior. In short, in biblical literature and tradition, the notion of the Son of Man was much vaguer and more uncertain than that of the Messiah. Jesus could freely speak of himself as the Son of Man without fearing accusations of anti-Roman rebellion and blasphemy, as the Scripture itself gave various meanings to this name. As for the common people, who were not knowledgeable in the Scripture's details, unlike the authorities and priests, they did not see any difference between these names. This attitude became firmly fixed in the books of the New Testament where, in contrast to the Old Testament, the terms Messiah and Son of Man are essentially identical.

Jesus's disciples

All the preachers and teachers of the law in Judea had many followers. Jesus, too, was in need of followers for the completion of his earthly mission. The gospels do not tell the same story about how Jesus gained his first students: While the Synoptic Gospels (those of Mark, Matthew, and Luke) assert that Jesus himself chose his closest helpers, the Gospel of John states the opposite—that John the Baptist's followers, such as Andrew, decided to join Jesus after their teacher revealed to them Christ's true nature. However, it is most likely that all the gospels are correct: Jesus both chose his disciples and accepted those who had followed John.

The area of Kinneret in the time of Jesus.
El-Araj - the most likely place of Bethsaida.

What guided Jesus when he chose his helpers? He was not interested at all in the person's literacy, social status, or wealth. The primary criteria were peoples' spiritual qualities, their ability to grasp the idea of the kingdom of God, and readiness for self-sacrifice—for the sake of preaching about the Lord's kingdom. It was because of this that sincere and straightforward commoners, who believed unconditionally in Jesus and in the world he represented, gathered around him. There were not amid his circle any learned scribes, experts on scripture, or the rich and powerful of this world. These commoners were from Galilee—the northern part of Judea of that time, particularly from the Lower Galilee, adjacent to Lake Kinneret (Sea of Galilee). All of them, like Jesus, were Jews, and their count—twelve—was by no means a coincidence. Jesus wanted to have the same number of disciples as there were Hebrew tribes. "Jesus said to them, 'Truly I tell you, at the renewal of all things, when the Son of Man sits on his glorious throne, you who have followed me will also sit on twelve thrones, judging the twelve tribes of Israel'" (Matthew 19:28). In this way, he emphasized his connection with Israel's history and biblical tradition. But who exactly are these elects of Jesus? To start, among them were three pairs of brothers: Peter (known as Simeon, or Kepha) and his brother Andrew; James and John, the sons of Zebedee; Jude (also known as Judas Thaddaeus, or Lebbaeus) and James, sons of Alphaeus. Then followed the "singles": Philip, Thomas (known as Didymus—Greek for "twin"), Bartholomew, Matthew, Simon Cananeus (known as Simon the Zealot), and finally, Judas Iscariot.

It should be noted that several disciples are known by other names in the New Testament writings. For instance, in the Gospel of Mark, Jude, brother of James, son of Alphaeus, is called "Thaddaeus" (Mark 3:18); the Gospel of Matthew gives him that name as well (Matthew 10:2−4). At the same time, the Gospel of Luke and the Acts of the Apostles refer to him as "Judas son of James" (Luke 6:16, Acts 1:13), while the Gospel of John calls him simply "Judas (not Judas Iscariot)" (John 14:22). All this brings considerable confusion, but it is not accidental. After all, among the twelve disciples of Jesus were two Simons, two Jameses, and two Judases; therefore, so as not to confuse them, they were given second names and nicknames. To distinguish between the two Simons, Jesus gave one of them the nickname Peter (for "rock" in Greek or kepha/cephas in Aramaic)—while the other was called Cananeus—by the name of his native town Cana, the very place where Jesus had turned water into wine. But since Simon Cananeus used to be a Zealot—an ardent supporter of the Jewish radical group that fought the Romans for Judea's freedom—he was given an epithet, the Zealot.

The case of the two Jameses was easier: to their names were added their fathers' names; thus appeared James, son of Zebedee, and James, son of Alphaeus. As for the two Judases, nicknames were resorted to again: one became Judas the Iscariot, while the other, Jude, was given two names— Thaddaeus and Judas, son of James. Finally, after Jesus's crucifixion, there appeared a second Matthew; he was chosen to be the twelfth apostle in lieu of Judas Iscariot. In order to distinguish him from the other Matthew, he was given a Greek version of that name—Matthias.

At the same time, we do not know the true name of Thomas, who was called the "twin." The fact is that the name Thomas is merely a distorted transliteration of the Hebrew and Aramaic word, *te'om* (twin). The Greek version of this name—Didymus—likewise means "twin." But what was the actual name of this disciple who was called this?

Unclear is the role of another follower of Jesus—Nathaniel. None of the three Synoptic Gospels include him as one of Jesus's twelve disciples; actually, they make no mention of him at all. In contrast, the Gospel of John depicts Nathaniel as one of Jesus's closest disciples. It was about this very Nathaniel that Jesus said: "Here truly is an Israelite in whom there is no deceit" (John 1:47). He, like Simon Cananeus (the Zealot), was from Cana and became one of the first to follow Jesus. It was for him that Philip came to deliver the news: "We have found the one Moses wrote about in the Law, and about whom the prophets also wrote—Jesus of Nazareth, the son of Joseph." To which Nathaniel replied, with his famous phrase: "Nazareth! Can anything good come from there?" (John 1:45–46). Could Nathaniel, in reality, be the true name of the always doubtful apostle Thomas? The Gospel of John excludes this supposition with the following statement: "Simon Peter, Thomas (also known as Didymus), Nathanael from Cana in Galilee, the sons of Zebedee, and two other disciples were together" (John 21:2). Thus, we are left to assume that the Hebrew name Nathaniel belonged to a disciple who was called in the Synoptic Gospels by the Hellenized name Bartholomew. As is known, in the era of the domination of Hellenistic culture in the eastern Mediterranean, it was customary among the Jewish people to have two names—one's own (Jewish) and a second in Greek (Latin was less common) that was used for communication with the Greco-Roman world. The most renowned apostles, Peter and Paul, were actually named Shimon and Saul, respectively (their Jewish names). All of Jesus's disciples had both Jewish and Greek names. The problem is that, at times, the gospels mention either just the Jewish names or only the Greek names, which makes it difficult to identify some of the disciples. There is no doubt that Andrew, Peter's brother, as well as Philip, Bartholomew, and Thomas had their own Jewish names—just as the brothers James and John (sons of Zebedee), and Jude and James (sons of Alphaeus), as well as Judas Iscariot, could have had parallel Greek names. It should be taken into account that all Jewish personal names and the names of geographic locations were very Hellenized in the gospels. This was because copyists—usually Greeks who were natives of Asia Minor, Alexandria, or Syria—found it difficult to convey Jewish names and so tried to convert them to familiar Greek forms. After transliteration (letter-for-letter switches) into Greek, Hebrew names were transliterated into Latin, and much later were carried over into English. As a result of the three-stage transliteration, Jewish names changed drastically; for instance, Yochanan became John, Shimon became Simon, and the town Kfar Nahum became Capernaum. Not only that, the true name of Christ himself—Yoshua—became Jesus.

Mosaic boat of first-century C.E. found in Migdal (Lake Kinneret)

As the gospels testify, all of Jesus's disciples were from relatively small Galilean towns adjacent to Lake Kinneret. They included Capernaum, Bethsaida, and Cana. Half of Jesus's disciples were from Capernaum alone (this was also the place where Jesus started his preaching): Peter and his brother Andrew, as well as the Zebedee and Alphaeus brothers. The fact that absolutely all of them were Galileans is indirectly confirmed in the Acts of the Apostles, which, in characterizing the attitude of Jerusalem's residents to Jesus's disciples, wrote: "Utterly amazed, they asked: 'Aren't all these who are speaking Galileans?'" (Acts 2:7). But Mary Magdalene, who is mentioned in the gospels, was from there as well—from Galilee's ancient city Magdala.

The majority of Jesus's disciples were fishermen on Lake Kinneret and, as recognized by the Book of Acts, "were unschooled, ordinary men" (Acts 4:13). Admittedly, some of them were fairly wealthy people; for example, James and John Zebedee were sons of a rich fisherman who hired his own workers. Before joining Jesus, another apostle, Matthew, was known as a tax collector, and the nature of his work demanded sufficient literacy and availability of funds. In fact, it is because of his relative erudition that he is mistakenly credited with the authorship of the Gospel of Matthew. Another prosperous man was Jesus' secret disciple—Joseph of Arimathea, who later bought the body of Jesus from the Roman governor Pontius Pilate and acquired a burial cave.

Jesus had many followers. Luke the Evangelist talks of seventy disciples, whom Jesus sent in pairs to cities and towns where he himself wanted to go (Luke 10:1). But only twelve of these followers became his companions and comprised his circle. And of these twelve, three were considered closest to and most trusted by him: Peter and the Zebedee brothers—John and James. They had been the first to join Christ. Jesus had taken only them with him during the most important moments of his earthly life; he also gave them the most critical assignments. They, and not anyone else, witnessed the transfiguration of Jesus on Mount Tabor, as well as the resurrection of Jairus's daughter; these three were also present in Gethsemane on the eve of Jesus's arrest (Mark 9:2; 5:22–23, 37; 14:32–33). After his resurrection, Jesus entrusted one of them—Peter—with leadership over all the disciples and followers. It was to him that Jesus said, three times, in the presence of his disciples: "Take care of my sheep"—thereby letting them know that he appointed Peter as his successor (John 21:15–17). However, Jesus had singled out Peter well before the end of his earthly life. This was what Jesus said to him: "And I tell you that you are Peter, and on this rock I will build my church, and the gates of Hades will not overcome it. I will give you the keys of the kingdom of heaven; whatever you bind on earth will be bound in heaven, and whatever you loose on earth will be loosed in heaven" (Matthew 16:18–19).

It is likely that the apostle second closest to Jesus was John Zebedee, brother of James. According to the Gospel of John, only the apostle John, as a beloved disciple, "reclined next to him [Jesus]" during the Last Supper, and it was to John that Jesus showed who would betray him (John 13:23–26). He was the only one of all the disciples who was present at Christ's crucifixion, and was the first to enter the cave where Jesus's body had been left. John became the second (after Peter) to be permitted by Jesus to follow him after his third appearance before the disciples "since the resurrection from the dead" (John 19:26; 20:3–5; 21:20–22). Judging by the apostle Paul's writings, John Zebedee was considered one of the most authoritative and respected leaders of Jerusalem's Christian community, second in significance only to Peter and James, Jesus's brother. He is often identified with John the Evangelist, author of the Gospel of John, even though this assumption is incorrect.

Jesus loved John and James Zebedee, and "to them he gave the name Boanerges, which means 'sons of thunder'" (Mark 3:17). It is likely that of the two brothers, James was the elder; that is why in all the gospels the name James appears before John. Seeing Jesus's favorable attitude to them, the brothers even asked him for a special privilege: "Let one of us sit at your right and the other at your left in your glory" (Mark 10:37). But while John lived a long and worthy life, his brother James was less fortunate. For an unknown reason, James Zebedee was executed by order of Agrippa I, even though the other apostles, and the Christian community in general, did not suffer. Since the early Middle Ages, there has been considerable confusion associated with the name of the apostle James. Many theologians and fathers of the Church believed that the name belonged to either James Zebedee, brother of John, or James Alphaeus. It was only in the last century that biblical studies finally established that the name actually referred to the brother of Jesus himself.

Although Jesus distinguished Peter and the Zebedee brothers (John and James) from among all his disciples, he was against any kind of hierarchy among them and believed that any attempt to elevate some at the expense of others must be condemned and punished. "Whoever wants to become great among you must be your servant, and whoever wants to be first must be slave of all" (Mark 10:43–44). Jesus responded to the

Zebedee brothers' request (to sit at his side) in this way: "but to sit at my right or left is not for me to grant. These places belong to those for whom they have been prepared" (Mark 10:40). But the disciples could not restrain themselves from vanity, and there was one time when "on the way they had argued about who was the greatest" (Mark 9:34). The fact that they were at different levels of closeness to Jesus in itself established some degree of hierarchy among them. The following episode testifies to this: "Now there were some Greeks among those who went up to worship at the festival. They came to Philip, who was from Bethsaida in Galilee, with a request. 'Sir,' they said, 'we would like to see Jesus.' Philip went to tell Andrew; Andrew and Philip in turn told Jesus" (John 12:20–22). Apparently, Andrew, as the brother of Peter, was closer to Jesus than Philip, but at the same time, was not one of Jesus's three closest disciples (who were Peter, John, and James).

Jesus required complete self-denial from his disciples. "If anyone comes to me and does not hate father and mother, wife and children, brothers and sisters—yes, even their own life—such a person cannot be my disciple" (Luke 14:26). When explaining his more than stringent demands, Jesus said: "No one who puts a hand to the plow and looks back is fit for service in the kingdom of God. . . . Those of you who do not give up everything you have cannot be my disciples" (Luke 9:62; 14:33). The disciples had to fully devote themselves to preaching about the Lord's word. Therefore, Jesus did not let one of them go when the latter wanted to bury his father, stating: "Let the dead bury their own dead, but you go and proclaim the kingdom of God," and he did not allow another to even say goodbye to his family (Luke 9:60–61). If these were the conditions that Jesus set forth for his disciples, then it would be reasonable to assume that none of them were married or had their own families. However, there is indirect proof that Peter was married, as Jesus had cured his mother-in-law of the fever (Mark 1:29–31). But nothing is said anywhere about Peter's wife or children. We do have one more piece of evidence, from Papias of Hierapolis, a father of the early Church, who claims that he knew the daughters of Philip (Jesus's disciple) well.

The twelve closest disciples of Jesus not only accompanied their Teacher everywhere but were also his "extraordinary and plenipotentiary messengers." According to the Gospel of Mark, Jesus, "calling the Twelve to him, began to send them out two by two and gave them authority over impure spirits . . . They went out and preached that people should repent. They drove out many demons and anointed many sick people with oil and healed them" (Mark 6:7, 12–13). From this, it is seen that Jesus recognized and used the possibility of mediation between man and God, between him and ordinary people.

Jesus sent his disciples not to everyone but rather to his own people. The Gospel of Matthew adds that Jesus, having sent the Twelve to preach, instructed: "Do not go among the Gentiles or enter any town of the Samaritans. Go rather to the lost sheep of Israel" (Matthew 10:5–6). That is, Jesus's preaching was directed exclusively to the Judeans, and he saw the meaning of his coming to this world in the salvation of the Jewish people.

However, not all of Jesus's followers accompanied him or contested the right to be his disciples. There is an interesting episode regarding this, given by Mark: "'Teacher,' said John, 'we saw someone driving out demons in your name and we told him to stop, because he was not one of us.' 'Do not stop him,' Jesus said. 'For no one who does a miracle in my name can in the next moment say anything bad about me'" (Mark 9:38–39).

But how did the disciples themselves treat their remarkable Teacher, and who did they take him to be? According to Mark, "Jesus and his disciples went on to the villages around Caesarea Philippi. On the way he asked them, 'Who do people say I am?' They replied, 'Some say John the Baptist; others say Elijah; and still others, one of the prophets.' 'But what about you?' he asked. 'Who do you say I am?' Peter answered, 'You are the Messiah'" (Mark 8:27–29). Likewise, an episode from Luke confirms that the disciples viewed Jesus as the Messiah—that is, the Savior who was to free Judea from the Romans' rule. "But we had hoped that he was the one who was going to redeem Israel" (Luke 24:21). So said his followers, who did not yet know of Jesus's resurrection. Jesus often tried to explain to his disciples that he was by no means the Messiah who, according to Jewish tradition, was to expel by force the Romans from Judea and ascend the throne of King David; he clarified that his kingdom was not on earth, but in the immaterial world of our Creator. Yet, he was met with confusion and misunderstanding. "He said to them, 'The Son of Man is going to be delivered into the hands of men. They will kill him, and after three days he will rise.' But they did not understand what he meant and were afraid to ask him about it" (Mark 9:31–32). Herein lay the main problem of Jesus's disciples: Very frequently, they failed to understand him, even though Jesus strove to talk to people as simply as possible and used parables. "He did not say anything to them without using a parable. But when he was alone with his own disciples, he explained everything" (Mark 4:34). The issue remained—even his closest disciples (Peter, James, and John) were not able to comprehend the meaning of Jesus's mission; they could not understand how the Savior, who was to achieve victory over all enemies, could instead become a victim of those very foes. It was even more difficult for them to grasp the idea of resurrection from the dead on the third day. The Pharisee movement in Judaism recognized the existence of an afterworld but said nothing of the possibility of resurrection from the dead, let alone on the third day.

The episode of Jesus's transfiguration on top of Mount Tabor testifies to how poorly the disciples understood him. Jesus had taken there only three of his disciples—Peter, James, and John, who were most devoted to him—so that they could better realize the true nature of Christ and his earthly mission; however, Jesus forbade them to say anything about what they had seen. The scene of Jesus's transfiguration in effect represented his contact with the world of our Creator. But all that we know of it comes from the confused impressions of the frightened disciples, who failed to comprehend what had occurred before them. Moreover, all this is related in the accounts of the evangelists, who had no firsthand knowledge of the event.

As further events showed, of all the disciples of Jesus, only Peter and John had a significant impact on the development of early Christianity; the role and contributions of the others went relatively unnoticed. This was no accident; after all, almost all of Jesus's twelve disciples were commoners from Galilee, people who were fairly illiterate and unlearned in the Scripture. But the torch that fell from the hands of the Twelve was picked up by others—Jews of the Diaspora, such as Paul, Barnabas, Mark, Silas, Luke, and John the Evangelist. Despite having never seen or heard Jesus himself, they became his true apostles. Unlike the twelve disciples, they were educated and well-read in the Scripture; they knew not only the Hebrew and Aramaic languages but Greek too. It was they, and others like them, who created the entire New Testament literature, including the canonical gospels.

Who was Mary Magdalene?

While narrating the crucifixion, burial, and resurrection of Jesus, the gospels single out Mary Magdalene from the group of women who came with Jesus from Galilee. She is not merely noted among the rest but put in first place, ahead of Jesus's mother. Furthermore, according to Mark and

John, the resurrected Jesus appeared first not to his disciples or mother but to Magdalene. John the Evangelist went even further in his gospel: He made Magdalene the main heroine in the scenes of the disappearance of Jesus's body and his resurrection on the third day after the crucifixion. What caused this kind of attention to her, and why is it that, in three gospels, Magdalene's name appears before that of Jesus's mother? As a rule, in the ancient world such an honor could have been given only to a wife. Can it then be possible that those who made the bold, and in some cases cynical conjecture that Mary Magdalene was Jesus's wife, or was at least intimate with him, were correct? Well, there is not the slightest hint of any relations between Jesus and Magdalene in any of the gospels. All insinuations on this matter are based solely on the Apocrypha—fictions of former pagans that were fabricated hundreds of years after Jesus's crucifixion. In reality, we have very little information about Mary Magdalene. We know only that she came from the city of Magdala, situated on the shore of Lake Kinneret in Galilee, and that Jesus drove out from her seven demons. That is all that we know for certain. The only information that can be added is that Magdala is very ancient—it is mentioned as a city in Canaan in the Amarna Letters, in the 14th century BC.

Magdalene's special role among the women who came from Galilee is explained in an entirely different way. Grateful for having been delivered from the demons, Mary Magdalene began to help the Teacher and his disciples. Evidently, she became not just a companion of Jesus but also the first female disciple. And Jesus put all his disciples and followers above his own relatives. He frequently stated: "For whoever does the will of my Father in heaven is my brother and sister and mother," and "pointing to his disciples, he said, 'Here are my mother and my brothers'" (Matthew 12:49–50).

As is known, none of Jesus's disciples were present at his crucifixion and burial (except for John, if we are to believe the account of John the Evangelist). All of them, afraid to share the fate of their Teacher, fled or hid. Magdalene alone was loyal to Jesus to the very end; it was she who brought the grief-stricken women to Jesus's execution and sent everyone to the burial cave at the end of the Sabbath. Given the circumstances, it is not so surprising that Jesus appeared first to Magdalene and not to Peter, his closest disciple, who had abandoned him three times on the night of the arrest alone. Memories of Magdalene's courage and loyalty secured her, in the gospels, first place among the women who had come from Galilee.

The further fate of Mary Magdalene is, again, unknown to us. According to some rather late sources, she died in Ephesus (Asia Minor), being there with Mary—the mother of Jesus. Other accounts, which are even more unreliable, claim that Magdalene found her last home in Provence (currently, southern France). Her native city Magdala, as well as neighboring Capernaum, Bethsaida, and Cana—the places where Jesus's disciples were from—were destroyed by the Romans during the Great Jewish Revolt (66–73 CE).

Mary Magdalene as a Hermit. A painting of Francesco Hayez. 1833.

The attitude of the Eastern and Western churches to this Jewish woman is quite interesting. If in Orthodoxy she had begun to be revered as a saint, in Catholicism she was much less fortunate. There, Magdalene was consistently confused with other women mentioned by the gospels: she was mistaken either for Mary, sister of Martha and Lazarus from Bethany (John 12:1–3), or for an unknown woman, who poured on Jesus's head a very expensive perfume (Matthew 26:6–7). But in most cases, Magdalene was identified with yet another woman, one "who lived a sinful life, wiped the feet of Jesus with her hair, kissed them and poured perfume on them" (Luke 7:37–38). Some believed that all three of these female characters represented the same Magdalene. Gradually, Western European peoples' perception of Mary Magdalene became associated erroneously with the image of a repentant, loose woman with an alabaster jar—containing anointing oil—in her hands. And although today the Roman Catholic Church has recognized this mistake (while the

Protestants never made it), changing the received view of Magdalene has proven to be difficult.

Related to her name is a legend, according to which Mary Magdalene was received by Emperor Tiberius during her stay in Rome. When she told him of Jesus's resurrection, he did not believe her and stated that the occurrence was as impossible as having the egg that he held in his hand turn red. At that very moment, the egg became completely red. This legend appeared in Europe fifteen hundred years after Jesus's crucifixion and was, of course, entirely mythical.

The Pharisees

In Judea of Jesus's time, all the most authoritative teachers of the law, including Hillel the Elder, Shammai, and Gamaliel I, were of the Pharisees. Their views were shared to no small extent by John the Baptist and Jesus himself. The majority of Christ's disciples, and later the apostle Paul, likewise were connected to the Pharisees. In spite of this, the controversies Jesus had with this religious group are clearly highlighted in all the gospels. Jesus highly criticized the proponents of this—and not any other—movement of Judaism. When speaking of the Pharisees, he quoted the words of the prophet Isaiah: "These people honor me with their lips, but their hearts are far from me. They worship me in vain; their teachings are merely human rules" (Matthew 15:8–9). Jesus called them " . . . blind guides. If the blind lead the blind, both will fall into a pit" (Matthew 15:14). He accused them of treating the laws of Judaism not in essence but in form, thereby emasculating their meaning. Jesus viewed them as hypocrites, who taught people one thing, but themselves did another. They "have let go of the commands of God and are holding on to human traditions" (Mark 7:8).

Both Jesus and the Pharisees shared and defended the laws of Moses. The essence of their disagreements lay in determining which of these laws were primary and which secondary. Jesus gave preference to the Written Torah (Pentateuch)—that is, the "laws of God"—while the Pharisees put before all else the Oral Torah that comprised, as Jesus determined, the "laws of man," which often were not even followed. But it was the Oral Torah that was most difficult for people to adhere to and fulfill. Without objecting to what the Pharisees taught, Jesus would say to his followers: "The teachers of the law and the Pharisees sit in Moses' seat. So you must be careful to do everything they tell you. But do not do what they do, for they do not practice what they preach. They tie up heavy, cumbersome loads and put them on other people's shoulders, but they themselves are not willing to lift a finger to move them" (Matthew 23:2–4).

Most often, clashes between Jesus and the Pharisees occurred with respect to the rules of the observance of the Sabbath. As is known, one of the ten Sinai commandments that Moses received from God established the seventh day of the week, Saturday, as the day of rest for all. In the Pentateuch, the laws pertaining to the observance of the Sabbath are not specified. In the Oral Torah, however, they are elaborated in great detail. Thus, Jesus regarded them as rules invented by man. While the Pharisees maintained that Saturday existed for God, Jesus claimed the opposite: "The Sabbath was made for man, not man for the Sabbath" (Mark 2:27). Therefore, man should not suffer on the Sabbath for the observance of laws created for this day by people themselves.

The arguments also concerned dietary and hygienic rules, which, according to the Oral Torah, the Jews were to abide by. The Pharisees insisted on the scrupulous observance of each ritual; however, Jesus paid attention not to the washing of hands and composition of food but to one's words and actions. "Don't you see that nothing that enters a person from the outside can defile them? For it doesn't go into their heart but into their stomach, and then out of the body" (Mark 7:18–19). He believed that people were defiled not by what entered them but by what came from within them. "What comes out of a person is what defiles them. For it is from within, out of a person's heart, that evil thoughts come" (Mark 7:20–21).

At the same time, Jesus admitted that among the Pharisees and scribes were many righteous people who were close to the kingdom of God (Mark 12:32–34). One of them was the Pharisee Nicodemus, who is mentioned in detail on the Gospel of John (John 3:1–12).

Jesus' severe condemnation of those Pharisees who distorted the essence of Judaism's laws and did not undertake the very things that they called upon others to do was, to a significant degree, exaggerated by the authors of the gospels. After all, the Pharisees became the main ideological opponents of the first Christians. The furious polemics between these two were explained by their common spiritual heritage—the Old Testament (Tanakh), and by the fact that early Christianity basically grew out of the Pharisaic movement of Judaism. As always in history, the most heated debates occur between supporters of the closest ideologies. Exasperated by this struggle, the New Testament writings turned the name *Pharisee* into a synonym for hypocrite.

PART TWO

The path to the cross and new hope

The conspiracy

News of the miracles performed by Jesus quickly spread throughout all of Judea. But the most impressive wonder occurred in Bethany, a small village on the outskirts of Jerusalem. There, before the eyes of many people, Christ resurrected Lazarus, who had died and already been buried. As the Gospel of John narrates, Jesus, ignoring the warning of the sister of the deceased that "by this time there was a bad odor, for he [Lazarus] has been there four days," ordered the rock covering the entrance of the cave where Lazarus was buried to be moved (John 11:39). Having thanked the Lord for hearing him, "Jesus called in a loud voice, 'Lazarus, come out!' The dead man came out, his hands and feet wrapped with strips of linen, and a cloth around his face" (John 11:43–44). This miracle struck everyone; it was discussed at every corner in Jerusalem, and on the eve of Pesach (Passover), the capital of Judea recognized Jesus as the long-awaited Messiah. "Now the crowd that was with him when he called Lazarus from the tomb and raised him from the dead continued to spread the word. Many people, because they had heard that he had performed this sign, went out to meet him" (John 12:17–18). The Jews, both residents of Jerusalem and pilgrims, who had come to the Temple on the eve of the holiday, "took palm branches and went out to meet him, shouting, 'Hosanna!' 'Blessed is he who comes in the name of the Lord!' 'Blessed is the king of Israel!'" (John 12:13). After the incredible miracle involving

Lazarus, the people found hope and believed that the One, who was to free their country from the Romans and ascend the throne of King David, had finally come. That is why they began to glorify Jesus as the Messiah. Even the Pharisees admitted that "the whole world has gone after him!" (John 12:19). Christ had previously hidden from the authorities and the people his true mission, but this jubilation caused him to experience contradictory feelings: "Now my soul is troubled, and what shall I say? 'Father, save me from this hour'? No, it was for this very reason I came to this hour" (John 12:27). Jesus understood that as soon as the Romans and their appointees saw in him the Messiah, his earthly path would come to an end; they would view him as the "king of the Jews" who was to deprive them of power. If even his own disciples could not comprehend what it meant to be an untraditional Messiah and suffer at the hands of the people, then what was to be expected of the Romans and priests?

Pontius Pilate, Roman procurator of Judea at the time, treated with great suspicion every preacher who was influential among the people. Knowing the freedom-loving disposition of the Judeans and their rejection of pagan authority, he feared—and not without reason—that any religious movement could sooner or later grow into a revolt against the Romans. This is why he forced Herod Antipas to arrest and then to execute John the Baptist. And although the gospels blame only Herodias, the wife of Herod Antipas, for the death of John, the point of view of the historian Flavius Josephus—who was almost a contemporary of those events—seems more convincing. Josephus claims that the authorities' fear of John's influence over the people constituted the main reason for his execution. Jesus's miracles, however, agitated the Roman procurator even more than John's preaching. After all, Christ, like all his disciples, came from Galilee, the heart of the Jewish resistance to Rome. First the rumors and then the growing belief that Jesus was the Messiah who was to drive the Romans out of Judea deprived the procurator of sleep and peace. He demanded that the chief of the Roman garrison in Jerusalem and the high priest Caiaphas capture and bring to him for questioning the "king of the Jews."

Jerusalem, like most of Judea, was under the exclusive jurisdiction of the Romans, but they were careful not to enter the Temple grounds unnecessarily. Caiaphas found himself in a difficult position. On the one hand, he could not disobey the Romans, who had in fact appointed him to the post of high priest; on the other hand, he was afraid "there may be a riot among the people" (Mathew 26:5). After all, Jesus, feeling the support of the Jews, drove out all the merchants from the Temple and ruled there as if he was at home. Further actions of Caiaphas are described in the Gospel of John as follows:

> Then the chief priests and the Pharisees called a meeting of the Sanhedrin. "What are we accomplishing?" they asked. "Here is this man performing many signs. If we let him go on like this, everyone will believe in him, and then the Romans will come and take away both our temple and our nation." Then one of them, named Caiaphas, who was high priest that year, spoke up, "You know nothing at all! You do not realize that it is better for you that one man die for the people than that the whole nation perish." (John 11:47–50)

So Caiaphas, fearing the general revolt of the Jews and the merciless reaction of Rome, decided to prevent these misfortunes by betraying Jesus to Pontius Pilate. Perhaps the Pharisees, unlike the high priest appointed by the Romans, feared not for their own well-being but for the fate of their people, who, in the event of the defeat of the rebellion, would be doomed to destruction and dispersion. In any case, the above episode from the gospel shows that it was not disbelief in Jesus as the Messiah that caused the servants of Rome to plot against him but fear of him as the coming king of the Jews, who would lead the whole people against them.

Betrayal

The plot against Jesus was hatched not only by his enemies. Among the disciples of Christ, too, there was a man who had his own plans for the Teacher. Little is known about the traitor Judas Iscariot. Biblical scholars explain his nickname, Iscariot, in different ways. There is a view that it was given according to the place of birth, *ish-Kerayot* (man from Kerayot). After all, the other disciple, Simon from Cana, was called Cananeus. However, much more plausible is the notion that his nickname was given according to his occupation or beliefs. If so, then the name Iscariot derives from *sicarii* (dagger men), the name given in Judea to fanatics who were ready, for the sake of expelling the Romans, to go to even the most desperate lengths. This interpretation is supported by the fact that the other disciple of Jesus mentioned above, Simon the Cananeus, had another nickname – the Zealot, as fighters for the freedom of Judea were called. Consequently, among the disciples of Christ were two men known to have fought against the Romans with arms in their hands, Simon the Cananeus, nicknamed the Zealot, and the other Judas, son of (a different) Simon, nicknamed Iscariot. Both the Zealots and Sicarii were supporters of exclusively forceful methods of fighting against the Roman pagans. The Sicarii differed from the Zealots by only one thing—extreme fanaticism and a readiness to indiscriminately sacrifice both their own and other's lives for the sake of liberation from Roman rule.

Joining Jesus's disciples changed Judas Iscariot's attitude toward violence, but it did not reconcile him to the pagan Romans. Convinced that his teacher was the Messiah for whom the Jewish people were waiting, he hoped for the near liberation of the country from the power of foreigners. But all attempts to push Jesus to destroy his enemies were met with an insurmountable obstacle—the rejection by Christ of any actions leading to death and destruction. Like the rest of the disciples, the former "dagger" could not understand that Jesus came to our world not to destroy people but to save their immortal souls; this was how Jesus differed from traditional notions of the Messiah. Iscariot therefore decided to take an extreme measure: to force Christ to turn his power on his enemies. He hoped that the arrest of Jesus would cause him to incinerate the Romans and their servants—the priests of the Temple and the Herodians. So, when he learned that the high priest and his entourage were looking for an occasion to hand Jesus over to the Romans, he offered them his services.

There is a widespread misconception in Christian literature that Iscariot's betrayal was motivated by greedy interest, namely that the traitor was seduced by thirty pieces of silver. In fact, the three canonical gospels—Mark, Luke and John—not only do not confirm this, they do not even give reason to think so. Mark, Luke, and John speak only of the fact of Iscariot's betrayal, but they do not blame him for any greedy motives (Mark 14:10; Luke 22:3–5; John 13:27–30; 18:2–3). Luke and John explain the fact of betrayal only by the fact that "Satan entered into him" (John 13:27). "Satan entered Judas, called Iscariot" (Luke 22:3).

However, Luke and Mark add that the high priest was ready to reward the services of the traitor, although Iscariot did not ask for it. The apostle Paul, the author of the earliest New Testament writings, never mentioned the traitor anywhere, much less his selfish considerations. Where did the fault of greedy interest come from? It came only from the Gospel of Matthew (Matthew 26:14–15). However, this claim does not stand up to any criticism. We must not forget that Judas Iscariot was the treasurer of Christ and his disciples. He always had a box with the common money, and all donations were kept there (John 12:6; 13:29). Having the absolute trust of Jesus and his disciples, he could take any amount of money freely, so he did not need the notorious thirty pieces of silver. If he had wanted, he had access to much larger sums. In general, the Sicarii, despite their fanaticism and extremism, were considered not only courageous people but, more importantly, deeply honest, a kind of disinterested party. And how could it be otherwise: those who were ready, without hesitation, to give their lives for the freedom of others did not know self-interest. The fact that Christ himself chose Judas Iscariot as their common treasurer is itself evidence of the honesty and unselfishness of this man. To doubt the choice of Jesus would be to cast a shadow on the nature and purpose of Christ. All this suggests that it was not greed that was the real reason for the betrayal. How did this ridiculous accusation appear in the Gospel of Matthew? Most likely, it was added by the first copyists in the second century. They considered it necessary to portray the traitor in the most unflattering light so that his name would become synonymous with betrayal in general. And they succeeded, although it was achieved by very unworthy means.

The Last Supper by Leonardo da Vinci. 1490s.

But what exactly was the essence of Iscariot's betrayal? After all, Jesus did not do anything illegal and did not hide from anyone. Here we come to an important point that is usually ignored in the gospels. It turns out that Christ enjoyed not only the support but also the protection of the Jewish people. Because of this, he entered Jerusalem in triumph and ruled the Temple as if it were his home. Neither the Roman legionaries nor the servants of the high priest dared to touch him, fearing the indignation and revolt of the Jews. Jesus was perfectly safe as long as he was among the people, so his enemies were looking for a moment when the "king of the Jews" would be alone or with only his disciples. It was for this reason that a traitor was needed who would tell when and where the Messiah could be captured without fear of the wrath of the Judean people. Therefore Iscariot, according to the Gospel of Luke, "watched for an opportunity to hand Jesus over to them when no crowd was present" (Luke 22:6).

Probably to conceal his plan and lull the vigilance of the high priest and the Romans, Iscariot expressed his willingness to take the money offered to him. However, the plan of Sicarii to radicalize Jesus failed —Jesus preferred a painful execution on the cross rather than use his power for destructive purposes. After the dagger man realized that Christ would not destroy his enemies under any circumstances, according to the Gospel of Matthew, he "was seized with remorse and returned the thirty pieces of silver to the chief priests and the elders. 'I have sinned,' he said, 'for I have betrayed innocent blood'" (Matthew 27:3–4). Iscariot tried to beg forgiveness for his Teacher, but neither the Roman procurator nor the high priest was interested in the truth; they were interested only in the speedy execution of the king of the Jews. Their response to Sicarii's confession and pleas is remarkable: "What is that to us?" they replied. "That's your responsibility" (Matthew 27:4). According to Matthew, Iscariot, not having achieved the liberation of Christ, threw the pieces of silver to the high priest and committed suicide. Thus, if we follow the logic of the version of the same Matthew, then the "greed" of Judas Iscariot is not confirmed in any way, and the short phrase about his desire to get money for betrayal falls out from the general fabric of the story as a later addition.

As for the money thrown away, "the chief priests picked up the coins and said, "It is against the law to put this into the treasury, since it is blood money" (Matthew 27:6). According to one version, "they decided to use the money to buy the potter's field as a burial place for foreigners" (Matthew 27:7); according to another, they tried to give it to the poor. But when Jewish beggars learned of their origin, they also refused them. In the end, thirty pieces of silver were transferred to the treasury of the murderer of Christ—Pontius Pilate. He and only he accepted them without any objections.

The newly discovered Gospel of Judas offers an entirely new view of Iscariot. According to this perspective, Judas Iscariot was the closest and most beloved disciple of Jesus. It was Judas who understood the Teacher best and, at his insistence, helped him to get rid of the physical body that had become a trap for him in our material world. Thus, the betrayal of Jesus by Iscariot is considered an act committed by the will of Christ himself.

It should be noted at once that the Gospel of Judas was written not by Iscariot himself but by an unknown author around the middle of the second century, that is, much later than the four canonical gospels. Further, it is not just an apocrypha but a Gnostic work. Gnosticism—the first serious heresy in Christianity—considered premature death as a release for the righteous soul because the physical body is a trap for the soul. Once it finds itself in the mortal body, the soul suffers in our terrible earthly world, and to help its release was considered by the Gnostics a "benefaction." This is how Iscariot's act was evaluated. But neither Jesus nor his disciples were Gnostics. Moreover, Christ's earthly mission was far from complete, and Iscariot had not set out to free the spirit of Jesus but to turn all his power against the Romans. As for the will of Christ himself, we should recall his words about the traitor: "But woe to that man who betrays the Son of Man! It would be better for him if he had not been born" (Mark 14:21). In general, the Gnostic character of the Gospel of Judas and the rather late time of its writing greatly devalue this work and turn it into an ordinary apocryphon.

Arrest

From the episode of Jesus's arrest to his crucifixion, all four canonical gospels contain a considerable number of insertions and distortions made by second-century copyists. But those who considered it necessary to "correct" the original texts of the gospels had no idea of the situation in Judea in the '20s of the first century CE, so their "additions" are serious historical errors. A major error concerns claims that the soldiers and servants of the high priest arrested Jesus. But Caiaphas could not arrest anyone; moreover, he didn't even have an armed guard of his own. Unlike Galilee, Perea, and southern Syria, which were under the rule of the sons of Herod the Great, Jerusalem, like all of Judea, was under the exclusive jurisdiction of the Romans, and only they could carry weapons and make arrests there. The authority of the high priest extended only to the territory of the Temple in Jerusalem. True, he could, at the request of the Romans, give them his unarmed servants, and most importantly Iscariot, as a guide, which in fact he did. The famous traitor's kiss is further proof that Roman soldiers, not Jews, captured Jesus in the Garden of Gethsemane. After the solemn reception of Jesus in Jerusalem and his sermons in the Temple, the Jews knew Jesus by sight and did not need the kiss of Iscariot to find their Teacher among the disciples. But the Roman legionnaires, who had never seen or heard the Jewish Messiah, did.

In the Gospel of Luke, there is an episode where the disciples, having gathered for the last time with Jesus in the Garden of Gethsemane, said to their Teacher: "See, Lord, here are two swords." "That's enough!" he replied" (Luke 22:38). Why did Christ's disciples need swords, and why were there only two? This seemingly incomprehensible episode actually sheds light on the arrest of Jesus. His disciples feared that after Jesus had taken charge of the Temple, the servants of the high priest might cause them all sorts of trouble and possibly threaten them. But the high priest's men were not allowed to carry weapons, so two swords were enough to counter any of their threats. With one of these swords, Peter cut off the ear of the high priest's servant (John 18:10). But when a group of Roman soldiers appeared behind Caiaphas's servants, these swords became useless, and the disciples of Jesus fled (Matthew 26:56; Mark 14:50). Those who captured Jesus are called "soldiers" in the Gospel of John, and their leader is called "the commander" (John 18:12). But apart from Romans, there could not have been any other soldiers in Jerusalem at that time, especially if we are talking about the "soldiers with its commander."

It is worth mentioning the words of Iscariot just before the arrest of Jesus: "The one I kiss is the man; arrest him and lead him away under guard" (Mark 14:44). Biblical scholars have made a lot of assumptions about what the phrase "under guard" might mean. For example, a renowned expert of New Testament writings, Bart Ehrman, believed that Iscariot may have been concerned for the life and safety of his Teacher. However, much more likely is a completely different explanation: The traitor was afraid that the Jews, having heard about the arrest of Jesus in whom they saw the Messiah or prophet, might attack the Romans on the way and free him.

Having forbidden Peter to engage in senseless resistance, Jesus speaks the words that Judas Iscariot most expected and for which he committed betrayal: "Put your sword back in its place," Jesus said to him, "for all who draw the sword will die by the sword. Do you think I cannot call on my Father, and he will at once put at my disposal more than twelve legions of angels?" (Matthew 26:52–53). However, neither Peter nor Iscariot was able to understand that Jesus would never raise up legions of angels to sow death and destruction, for he came not to judge but to save.

A trial that didn't happen

Where was Jesus taken after his arrest? First to the high priest Caiaphas. However, the Gospel of John makes a small correction: Before getting to the high priest, Jesus was taken to Anna, the father-in-law of the high priest and only then to Caiaphas himself. Further versions of the gospels differ from each other. The Gospels of Mark and Matthew state that the same night (!) the supreme religious court—the Sanhedrin—was convened, which immediately (!) decided on the guilt of Jesus and on his transfer to the Romans. The Gospel of Luke does not confirm this haste and says that the meeting of the Sanhedrin took place only the next day. But the Gospel of John does not mention any trial at all and reports that after a short meeting with Caiaphas, Jesus was immediately brought to the Roman procurator Pontius Pilate. What really happened? Was there a trial or not?

First of all, the version from Mark and Matthew about the immediate convocation of the court, and even at night, and about an equally quick decision on such a complex issue, is frankly implausible. It should not be forgotten that serious charges for which a death sentence could be imposed were to be discussed only by the Great Sanhedrin and only in its entirety, that is, in the presence of 71 people. Many of them were elderly and lived far from Jerusalem. It took at least a few days to call such a court. Even more time would have been needed for the trial and sentencing. It is worth recalling that the trial of the apostles Peter and John was able to take place the next day only because at the time of their arrest it was already evening. But they were judged by only a Small Sanhedrin of 23 people. And an incomparably simpler question was discussed: how the apostles cured a man who was lame from birth. Despite this, the debate in court dragged on for two days. As for Jesus, he was captured at night, when there was no question of any meeting of the Sanhedrin. The charge against him was considered incomparably more serious than that brought against the apostles, so without the convocation of the Great

Sanhedrin, Jesus could not be sentenced. Thus, if the trial of Christ had actually taken place, it would have taken at least a week.

However, the actual problem was different. From the point of view of the laws of Judaism, the confession of Jesus that he is the Messiah could not be considered a crime at all, at least until the case was considered in court. The Sanhedrin would demand evidence, and only if Jesus refused to present it would he be charged and sentenced accordingly. So, everything depended on the court's decision. But among the members of the Sanhedrin, there were many who sympathized with Jesus and secretly supported him—for example, the Pharisee Nicodemus, Joseph of Arimathea, and even the famous teacher of the law, Gamaliel the Elder. They would have done anything to get the Sanhedrin to acquit Jesus or limit itself to a lenient sentence. In any case, the high priest could not be sure of the outcome of the Sanhedrin session. But Caiaphas feared more than that. He was afraid of the unpredictable reaction of the Jewish people, who had high hopes for Jesus. After all, according to the gospels, Jesus could not be captured either in the Temple or in the streets of Jerusalem because of fear of the Jews, who defended him and "held that he was a prophet" (Mark 12:12; Matthew 21:46; Luke 22:2; 19:47–48). Every day of delay threatened popular unrest and a clash with the Romans, so Caiaphas decided not to waste time by contacting the Sanhedrin.

Thus, we have every reason to believe that it was not by chance that the Gospel of John did not mention the judgment of the Sanhedrin; it simply did not exist. Moreover, the high priest did not even intend to call a supreme court, either the Great or Small, because he was afraid that it might take too long and end in the acquittal of Jesus. The legionaries brought Christ to Caiaphas not to organize the trial of the Sanhedrin but to get the high priest's permission to transfer Jesus into the hands of the Roman procurator. Not wanting to irritate the Jews by interfering in their religious disputes, they wanted to secure the formal consent of Caiaphas, as the main Judean authority. Therefore, the so-called session of the Sanhedrin was really just a short interrogation by the high priest.

But if, from the point of view of the Jews, Jesus declaring himself the Messiah was not considered a deliberate crime, then why does the Gospel say that "the high priest tore his clothes" and "condemned Jesus as worthy of death"? (Mark 14:63–64). Here we come to the point. To recognize himself as the Messiah, that is, the king of the Jews, was a terrible crime in the eyes of the Romans and their servants—the high priest and his entourage. This was a challenge to Roman authority in Judea and was punishable by death on the cross. Therefore, the real trial did not take place in the Sanhedrin or even with Caiaphas but with the Roman procurator Pontius Pilate.

Pontius Pilate

Here we are faced with another distortion of the gospels, which was committed by the second-century copyists, namely, the positive image of the Roman procurator. Fortunately, we know about Pontius Pilate not only from the gospels but also from other historical sources. He was mentioned in the writings of Philo of Alexandria, Flavius Josephus, and Tacitus. Moreover, we even have archaeological evidence of the existence of such a historical figure: In 1961, an inscription of the first century CE with the names of the Roman emperor Tiberius and Pontius Pilate was discovered in Caesarea (Israel). Who was the Roman procurator of Judea?

Pontius Pilate could not boast of either aristocratic or Latin origin. His family belonged to the equestrian class, the second class of Roman society after the senators, and were part of the Samnite clan of the Pontii. As is known, since the 3rd century BC, many rich artisans and usurers joined the ranks of horsemen, so most members of this class were not of the nobility. In 26 CE, Emperor Tiberius appointed Pilate governor (26–36 CE) of Judea. This was done under the patronage of Sejanus, an influential court intriguer known for killing, poisoning, and torturing almost all the heirs of the ruling dynasty. At that time, the governor of Judea had a lower official rank, prefect, so Pilate was most likely a prefect, not a procurator. Pilate's contemporaries spoke of him as a hard-hearted and treacherous ruler, capable of committing any crime for his own benefit. He was the fifth governor of Judea but the first of them who dared to provoke the Jews into conflict. He began his reign by insulting the religious feelings of the Jews by ordering gilded shields with Roman symbols to be brought to Jerusalem. When the Jews asked for them to be removed from their sacred places, as Philo of Alexandria testifies, Pilate persisted because "he was a man of a very inflexible disposition, and very merciless as well as very obstinate." Then the Jews let it be known that they would send an embassy to the Emperor Tiberius with a complaint against the procurator:

This last sentence exasperated him in the greatest possible degree, as he feared least they might in reality go on an embassy to the emperor, and might impeach him with respect to other particulars of his government, in respect of his corruption, and his acts of insolence, and his rapine, and his habit of insulting people, and his cruelty, and his continual murders of people untried and uncondemned, and his never ending, and gratuitous, and most grievous inhumanity. (Philo of Alexandria, *Embassy to Gaius* XXXVIII (302)

In the end, the Jews decided to send a message to the emperor, who was known for his favor for them, and the effect of this letter exceeded all their expectations:

And he, when he had read it, what did he say of Pilate, and what threats did he utter against him! . . . for immediately, without putting any thing off till the next day, he wrote a letter, reproaching and reviling him in the most bitter manner for his act of unprecedented audacity and wickedness, and commanding him immediately to take down the shields and to convey them away from the metropolis of Judaea to Caesarea . . . . (Philo of Alexandria, *Embassy to Gaius* XXXVIII (304–5)

However, the episode with the shields was not the only conflict between Pontius Pilate and the local Jews. The next clash was over the procurator's attempt to break into the treasury of the Temple in Jerusalem. Having appropriated the public money for the construction of the aqueduct, he decided to build it at the expense of funds collected for donations to the Temple. According to Josephus, "at this the multitude had indignation; and when Pilate was come to Jerusalem, they came about his tribunal, and made a clamor at it. Now when he was apprized aforehand of this disturbance, he mixed his own soldiers in their armor with the multitude, and ordered them to conceal themselves under the habits of private men, and not indeed to use their swords, but with their staves to beat those that made the clamor" (Josephus, *Wars of the Jews* 2.9.4). However, the Roman legionaries either overdid it or had another, unspoken order, as a result of which many unarmed people who did not expect an attack from behind were killed. In general, masquerades with the disguise of soldiers in civilian clothes and manipulations with these obedient "crowds" were very characteristic of the methods of Pontius Pilate's rule, especially since the Syrians who served in the Roman garrison did not differ in appearance from the Jews.

Despite the fact that the first copyists managed to remove all the anti-Roman episodes from the gospels, some traces of them remained. One of them, in the Gospel of Luke, clearly testifies against Pilate: "Now there were some present at that time who told Jesus about the Galileans whose blood Pilate had mixed with their sacrifices" (Luke 13:1). This is a reference to pilgrims from Galilee who came to the Jerusalem Temple to make sacrifices for the sake of peace and the well-being of their families but were themselves victims of one of the provocations of the Roman procurator.

Another conflict with the locals, this time the Samaritans, was the last for Pilate in his career as a procurator. Here, his victims were hundreds of innocent Samaritans who gathered at their sacred Mount Gerizim to dig up the vessels allegedly buried by Moses. Pilate's crime was so egregious that even the consul and Roman governor in Syria, Lucius Vitellius, supported the Samaritans' complaint. In 36 CE, an angry Tiberius summoned Pilate to Rome. The procurator was accused of two crimes at once: executions without trial and embezzlement. But Pilate did not manage to see the emperor, and Tiberius died before his arrival in Rome, so the new emperor, Gaius Caligula, organized his trial. In 39 CE, the former procurator was found guilty of theft and murder, and the emperor ordered him to commit suicide. This is what the Roman procurator of Judea, who organized the arrest and execution of Jesus, was like.

The evolution of Christian views on the personality of Pontius Pilate is interesting. From the very beginning, when the memory of those events was still fresh, they laid the blame for the crucifixion of Christ only on the Roman procurator. Hatred for the murderer of Jesus gave rise to the apocrypha that told about the terrible fate of Pilate. One such legend, told by the father of the Church and the Roman historian Eusebius of Caesarea (263–340 CE), says that Pilate was exiled to Vienne in Gaul for his crimes, where the endless misfortunes that befell him forced him to commit suicide. According to another apocrypha, after the suicide of the former procurator, his body was thrown into the Tiber, but the river did not accept the scoundrel. Then his corpse was taken to Vienne to be drowned in the Rhone, but its waters also rejected the murderer. In the end, he was buried in one of the alpine lakes. Of course, all these apocrypha have nothing to do with reality; they only confirm the fact that the first Christians felt extreme hostility toward

Pilate, considering him the main culprit in the execution of Christ. However, as the copyists emptied the gospels of anti-Roman episodes and shifted the responsibility for the crucifixion of Jesus to the Jews, the attitude of Christians toward Pilate also changed. In fact, the Coptic and Ethiopian churches canonized Pontius Pilate and his wife. This is a direct result of serious misrepresentations in the gospels, which is exactly what the pro-Roman editors of New Testament writings were trying to achieve.

Pilate's very first question was the one that most concerned the Romans, not the Jews: "Are you the king of the Jews?" (Mark 15:2; Matthew 27:11; Luke 23:3; John 18:33). To recognize himself as the Messiah, that is, the "king of the Jews," was to defy Roman authority and accept his inevitable death on the cross. Therefore, Jesus, despite the fact that he declared himself the Messiah to the high priest, gives an evasive answer, which could be interpreted in different ways. In the Gospel of John, Jesus adds: "My kingdom is not of this world . . . my kingdom is from another place" (John 18:36). Then follow the words of Pilate, which are an undoubted insertion into the original text of the gospels of Luke and John: "I find no basis for a charge against this man" (Luke 23:4; John 18:38). How can a Roman procurator not find fault with a man if he does not deny that he is the Messiah, that is, the king of the Jews? Who among the Roman pagans had the slightest idea of the "kingdom of God" that Jesus had in mind? The words attributed to Pilate are as absurd as if in some province of the Russian Empire a man appeared who declared himself czar, and the governor there, instead of arresting him and sending him in chains to St. Petersburg, declares that he does not see his guilt. And this is the same Pilate who ordered the murder without trial of hundreds of innocent people suspected of only the slightest disobedience to the authorities! Moreover, Pilate claims Jesus's innocence before he can interrogate him. Obviously, those who added this episode to the gospels wanted to whitewash the Roman procurator, as well as the Romans in general, at any cost. Then there is another historical blunder: "Now it was the governor's custom at the festival to release a prisoner chosen by the crowd" (Matthew 27:15). In fact, such a custom never existed in Jerusalem. But in the Hellenistic and Roman cities, this custom was widely practiced, only, of course, not at Passover but at the festivals of the pagan gods. This error reveals the Roman or Hellenistic origin of the copyists who decided to edit the gospels, people who had no idea about life in Judea in the time of Jesus. But even if we assume that the Romans had introduced their custom in Jerusalem—to release one prisoner to the people—the Roman procurator could not free Jesus, the "king of the Jews," but could pardon Barabbas, an ordinary robber who did not claim to be the leader of the Jews against Rome. This unreliable episode is followed by another, even more dubious, and most importantly, illogical one: "The chief priests and the elders persuaded the crowd to ask for Barabbas and to have Jesus executed" (Matthew 27:20). How were the high priest and his entourage able to win over the people, who deeply hated and despised them as Roman's henchmen? But more importantly, how did those people who gathered in thousands at the preaching of Jesus and considered him to be at least one of the prophets, the people who joyfully met him in Jerusalem and supported him when he drove the merchants out of the Temple, suddenly completely change, obey the Roman servants, and demand Jesus's execution? There is a clear conflict between the texts of the gospels. On the one hand, the "crowd" shouts and demands the crucifixion of Jesus (Luke 23:23). On the other hand, right next to it, the text says: "A large number of people followed him, including women who mourned and wailed for him" (Luke 23:27). So what kind of people demanded the crucifixion of Jesus? The great multitude of Jews who "mourned and wailed for him" or the "crowd" of Roman soldiers in disguise? Obviously, the copyists who distorted the original texts of the gospels were concerned not with elementary logic but with demonizing the Jews. In the light of such a blatant contradiction, the quote from the Gospel of Matthew— "All the people answered, 'His blood is on us and on our children!'"—is perceived as nothing more than a blood libel against the Jewish people by an antisemitic Hellenist (Matthew 27:25). However, the author of the gospel had nothing to do with it. This antisemitic insertion was added much later and by people who had nothing in common with the authors of the gospels.

The pro-Roman corrections of the gospels created an entirely new image of Pontius Pilate as a kind-hearted official who sympathizes with Jesus and believes in his innocence. Only the pressure of the "bloodthirsty" Jews makes him agree to the execution of Christ. However, in actuality, everything looked very different. The Roman procurator, whose cunning and cruelty were noted even by his contemporaries, feared the growing influence of Jesus and viewed him as a potential enemy of Roman power in Judea. It was Pilate who organized the arrest and execution of Christ. It is very likely that the original texts of the gospels reflected this true story.

The Crucifixion

In the Gospel of John, under a pile of pro-Roman statements by self-appointed editors, one most interesting fact has survived—the high priest refused to execute Jesus, despite the permission of Pilate (John 18:31; 19:6). The high priest had the right of execution but on the condition that the death sentence be approved by the Roman procurator. This right was used to execute the Jew Stephen, the first canonized Christian. He was sentenced to death through stoning—the traditional Near Eastern execution. But the high priest did not dare to do the same with Jesus. Was there something like conscience or mercy awakened in Caiaphas? Unlikely, because the Roman appointees were not much different from their masters. The explanation has a completely different reason: Jesus was defended by the Jewish people, the same "large number of people followed him, including women who mourned and wailed for him" (Luke 23:27). Caiaphas knew that if he dared to touch Jesus, he would be stoned to death along with his entourage. Not only execution, any punishment of Jesus threatened Caiaphas with confrontation from his own people. The execution of Christ was necessary for the Roman procurator; that was the only way he could get rid of the "king of the Jews" and his influence on the people. In the case of John the Baptist, everything was simpler: the Romans managed to deal with the most influential preacher by the hands of the Jews themselves, with the help of the tetrarch Herod Antipas. This time, the Judean ruler, despite his dependence on the Romans, refused to execute Jesus, finding no fault in him (Luke 23:15). Caiaphas also refused to do so, though only out of fear of his own people. Pontius Pilate had no choice but to carry out his plan himself, and by the hands of the Romans to subject Jesus to a purely Roman execution—crucifixion.

In cases where it is not clear who committed a crime, the question is always asked: In whose interest was it? In this case, we have a clear answer—it was necessary for the Romans. They did not understand the nature of Jesus's teaching but feared that the "king of the Jews" might pose a direct threat to their power in Judea. The inscription they made over the cross of Jesus—"King of the Jews"—is the best evidence of what exactly Christ was accused of and who could be afraid of him. The Jews, having lost Jesus, in whom they wanted to see their Messiah, lost hope for deliverance from the power of Rome. Pro-Roman copyists, distorting the texts of the gospels, tried to whitewash the barbarity and cruelty of the Romans, and this despite the fact that they committed outrages against Jesus and crucified him. The copyists did not stint even on praising the

Roman executioner, the centurion, attributing to him the recognition of the divine origin of Jesus (Mark 15: 39).

According to the gospels, at the cross of Jesus stood his mother, his mother's sister (Mary Cleopas), Mary Magdalene (the one from whom Christ cast out demons), the mother of the sons of Zebedee (Salome), and "many women were there, watching from a distance. They had followed Jesus from Galilee to care for his needs" (Matthew 27:55). But where were his disciples? They hid, afraid to share the fate of the Teacher. However, John the Evangelist, claiming that his gospel was written by John Zebedee himself, mentions the presence of John Zebedee at the crucifixion and even claims that Jesus entrusted John with the care of his mother.

The gospels do not contradict but rather complement the story of Jesus's crucifixion. However, they represent Christ's state of mind in very different ways. If in the earliest Gospel of Mark, Jesus is depicted as confused, lonely, and abandoned by the Father, in the latest canonical Gospel of John, Christ is completely calm and confident that everything is happening as it should be. In the Gospels of Mark and Matthew, Jesus is terrified and grieved, his soul grieves mortally, but he still has the hope that "this cap" of suffering and physical death "might pass from him," that the Father's intervention may change the course of events (Mark 14:33–34, 36; Matthew 26:39). The fact that Jesus went to the crucifixion and then died on the cross in a complete confusion of feelings confirms his last appeal to the Father: *"Eloi, Eloi, lama sabachthani?"* (My God, my God, why have you forsaken me?) (Mark 15:34). There is so much pain and despair in these words that no one can have the shadow of a doubt that Jesus did not leave his earthly life in a state of peace of mind, as the Gospel of John wants to assure us. Probably, events could have developed differently, and Jesus, until the very end, relied on the intervention of the world, which sent him to preach to people. For shortly before his arrest, he said to his disciples: "Now is the time for judgment on this world; now the prince of this world will be driven out" (John 12:31). However, none of this happened. Perhaps Jesus was expecting the intervention of the Creator, who stopped the hand of Abraham with a knife raised over his son Isaac. But though the sacrifice of Isaac was stopped at the last moment, the sacrifice of Jesus took place. The words of Christ lead to the assumption that something did not happen at the crucifixion that should have, and the Lord—for a reason beyond our understanding—changed the fate of the earthly world, so that events began to develop in a completely different direction.

However, without the physical death of Jesus, his resurrection would have been impossible, and without the resurrection of Christ, people would have found neither faith in him nor hope for his kingdom of God. Thus, the fulfillment of Jesus's mission in our material world required the sacrifice of his earthly life.

Jesus from the early Christian Basilica of Sant' Apollinare Nuovo, Ravenna, Italy. 6th century.

The day of the crucifixion of Jesus fell on Friday, and with the sunset of the same day came the Sabbath, a sacred day for the Jews. According to Jewish custom, on the Sabbath, especially on Passover, it was forbidden to leave dead bodies unburied. And although the Romans usually kept the bodies of the crucified on crosses for many months (to intimidate others), here in Judea, they had to take into account the religious traditions of the Jews, so they allowed the executed to be buried on the same day. One of Jesus's followers, Joseph of Arimathea, obtained Pontius Pilate's permission to bury the body of Christ. However, given the well-known greed of Pilate, Joseph probably had to buy the body of Jesus for a considerable sum.

In Judea, it was the custom to bury the deceased not in the ground or in wooden coffins, but in caves or crypts. The bodies of the deceased were anointed with incense, such as balsam or myrrh, and wrapped in a shroud. Therefore, when the gospels tell us that as Mary stood weeping outside Jesus's burial place, "she bent over to look into the tomb and saw two angels in white" (John 20:11–12), this is a reference to a burial cave that served as a tomb. The entrance to such caves were often closed by a huge stone, too heavy sometimes for the efforts of several people. Of course, such tombs were not cheap, and not everyone could afford to buy them, but Joseph, being a rich man, bought one of these caves near Golgotha, the place of Jesus's execution. The burial of Christ was observed by the same women who had been at the crucifixion, but all the disciples, including Peter, were again absent. The Gospel of John adds that in addition to Joseph of Arimathea, the Pharisee Nicodemus also came to the burial, bringing spices—myrrh and scarlet (John 19:39). Meanwhile, the gathering darkness reminded the mourners of the coming of the Sabbath, and the funeral rites were interrupted until the end of the holy day. The entrance to the cave where the body of Jesus lay was closed with a large boulder, and everyone dispersed, overwhelmed with grief.

The Gospel of Matthew emphasizes that a guard was set at the cave the next day to prevent the disciples from "stealing" their Teacher's body (Matthew 27:62–66). However, the rest of the gospels do not mention any watch at all. If the terrified disciples were afraid to see their Teacher off on his last journey, then it is unlikely that they would think of stealing his body. If Peter, the most trusted and intimate of all the disciples of Jesus, was forced to renounce him three times on the night of his arrest, who else among them would dare to steal his body? Obviously, the mention of a guard at the cave was intended to remove any suspicion by an incredulous reader that Jesus's disciples had stolen his body.

The Resurrection

The resurrection of Jesus occupies the central place in Christianity. Without the resurrection of Christ, the Jewish sect of the Nazarenes would never have become a new world religion. How can we not remember the words of the apostle Paul: "If Christ has not been raised, our preaching is useless and so is your faith" (1 Cor. 15:14). And at the same time, despite its extreme significance, the narration of the resurrection of Jesus is the most confusing and problematic part of the New Testament writings. Here the gospels no longer complement each other but give different versions, which rule out each other. Difficulties in understanding what happened and how it happened begin with the end of the Sabbath, when the women, bringing incense, return to the cave to finish the funeral rites over the body of Jesus.

Who came to the burial cave of Jesus on the third day after his crucifixion? While the Gospels of Mark and Luke speak of the same group of women who were present at the crucifixion and burial, the Gospel of Matthew mentions only two of them—Mary Magdalene and "the other Mary," and John the Evangelist claims that only Magdalene came (Matthew 28:1; John 20:1). For his part, Mark reports the concern of the women: Who will roll away for them the huge stone that closes the entrance to the cave? (Mark 16:3). Thus, he casts doubt on Matthew's version that the tomb was guarded. Furthermore, according to Mark, Luke, and John, someone had already rolled the blocking stone away before the women arrived; according to Matthew, however, this huge boulder was pushed away by an angel who appeared before the women's eyes (Matthew 28:2). According to Mark and Matthew, the women see a young man (an angel) in the cave, who informs them that Jesus has risen (Mark 16:5–6; Matthew 28:5–6). According to Luke's version, there were not one but two angels in the cave; on the other hand, John claims that at first Magdalene did not see anyone at all (Luke 24:4, John 20:1–2).

What was the reaction of the women? Mark says that "trembling and bewildered, the women went out and fled from the tomb. They said nothing to anyone, because they were afraid" (Mark 16:8). However, Matthew and Luke report exactly the opposite: "filled with joy," the women announced this to all the disciples, who did not believe them (Matthew 28:8; Luke 24:9,11). Meanwhile, according to John, the lonely Magdalene runs only to Peter and John and says: "They have taken the Lord out of the tomb, and we don't know where they have put him!" These two disciples, in turn, run into the cave and see that everything is exactly as Magdalene said (John 20:2–8). Although Luke claims that only Peter came, according to Matthew and Mark, none of the disciples appeared (Luke 24:12; Matt. 28; Mark 16).

The appearance of Jesus to Mary Magdalene.
A painting of A.A. Ivanov. 1835.

To whom did Jesus first appear? Mark and John say that Christ appeared at first only to Magdalene, but Matthew and Luke do not confirm this. According to Matthew, Jesus first appeared to two women—Magdalene and "the other Mary"—returning from the cave, and according to Luke, the first to see Christ were two of his followers who were walking from Jerusalem to the village of Emmaus (Matthew 28:9; Luke 24:13–32). Finally, the apostle Paul, in his epistle to the Corinthians, states that Jesus first appeared to Cephas, that is, to Peter (1 Cor. 15:5).

Where did Jesus's appearances to the disciples take place? Luke reports that they occurred only in Jerusalem (Luke 24:33–36, 49–52). Mark and Matthew insist they were only in Galilee (Mark 16:7,14; Matthew 28:7,16–17). But according to John, Jesus appeared to all the disciples in Jerusalem, and to seven of them in Galilee, on the Lake of Kinneret (John 20:19,26; 21:1).

What is the meaning of all these discrepancies and even obvious contradictions in the gospel versions of the resurrection of Jesus? It is evidence that the authors of the gospels were not the disciples of Jesus, that they not only never saw him but were not even his contemporaries. The canonical gospels known to us came to light at least a few decades after the crucifixion of Christ, so they were written on the basis of the fragmentary and often contradictory testimonies of those who once saw and heard Jesus.

To reconstruct the most complete picture of the resurrection of Jesus, we must bear in mind that we cannot rely on the end of the Gospel of Mark. Today, most experts in the field of ancient Greek believe that the final part of this gospel, namely 16:9–20, was completed at least two centuries after the creation of the main document. Moreover, this final part of the Gospel of Mark is absent in Codex Sinaiticus—the oldest complete manuscript of the New Testament (dating to mid-fourth century CE). Perhaps it is not a deliberate distortion of the gospel but an attempt to somehow restore its final part, which was lost or may not have been written by Mark himself. Perhaps it was impossible in some eyes to let the Gospel of Mark end as follows: "Trembling and bewildered, the women went out and fled from the tomb. They said nothing to anyone, because they were afraid" (Mark 16:9).

The last chapters in the Gospels of John and Matthew are also problematic. Many biblical scholars are convinced that the epilogue of the Gospel of John (chapter 21) was added later, after the writing of the work itself. It is likely that those who made this addition were motivated by a desire to destroy the myth, spread among early Christians, that Jesus promised to return during the lifetime of John Zebedee. As for the Book of Matthew, the epilogue (chapter 28) has traces of a later revision. For example, the following words: "Therefore go and make disciples of all nations, baptizing them in the name of the Father and of the Son and of the Holy Spirit" (Matthew 28:19) could not have been written by the author of the gospel, since the Christian doctrine of the Trinity appeared much later. Thus, the final parts of the three gospels—Mark, Matthew, and John, which speak of the resurrection of Jesus, have certainly been revised and contain inserts from later times. This makes it very difficult to reconstruct the true story of the resurrection of Jesus and indicates a de facto distortion of the gospels' original texts.

Two of the gospels—Luke and John—report an interesting fact: The risen Jesus appeared completely different. He had changed so much that no one recognized him, not even his close friends and disciples, and he had new and extraordinary abilities. He could suddenly appear and disappear, enter through closed doors, and become invisible. John reports that Jesus came to his disciples "though the doors were locked" (John 20:19,26). Luke narrates the appearance of Christ to two of his followers, one of whom, Cleopas, was probably a relative of his mother. For almost a whole day, the followers of Jesus walked along the same road with him, telling him about the crucifixion of the Teacher and the strange disappearance of his body, but during all this time, they did not recognize Christ. It was only when they stayed in the village for the night "when he was at the table with them, he took bread, gave thanks, broke it and began to give it to them. Then their eyes were opened, and they recognized him, and he disappeared from their sight" (Luke 24:30–31).

Even more eloquent evidence of the new appearance of the risen Jesus is given in the Gospel of John. Weeping inconsolably over the disappearance of the body of Christ, Magdalene

> turned around and saw Jesus standing there, but she did not realize who it was. He asked her, "Woman, why are you crying? Who is it you are looking for?" Thinking he was the gardener, she said, "Sir, if you have carried him away, tell me where you have put him, and I will get him." Jesus said to her, "Mary." She turned toward him and cried out in Aramaic, "*Rabboni!*" (Teacher). Jesus said, "Do not hold on to me, for I have not yet ascended to the Father. Go instead to my brothers and tell them, "I am ascending to my Father and your Father, to my God and your God." (John 20:14–17)

Indirect evidence of the complete change in the appearance of Jesus can also be found in the following phrase, this time from the Gospel of Matthew: "Then the eleven disciples went to Galilee, to the mountain where Jesus had told them to go. When they saw him, they worshiped him; but some doubted" (Matthew 28:16–17). The fact that even some of the disciples, who knew him so well, doubted this was their Teacher suggests Christ had manifested a new, unusual appearance for them. It is worth remembering the appearance of Jesus to the seven disciples on Lake Kinneret, in Galilee:

> Simon Peter, Thomas (also known as Didymus), Nathanael from Cana in Galilee, the sons of Zebedee, and two other disciples were together. "I'm going out to fish," Simon Peter told them, and they said, 'We'll go with you." So they went out and got into the boat, but that night they caught nothing. Early in the morning, Jesus stood on the shore, but the disciples did not realize that it was Jesus. (John 21:2–4)

Why, in the three days since the crucifixion, had Jesus's appearance changed so much that no one recognized him? After all, Lazarus, who had been dead for four days, remained the same. Perhaps the world of our Creator, who resurrected and sent Jesus back to people, thought it necessary to exclude any possibility that the authorities and the uninitiated would learn the mysteries of the crucified Christ. Given that Jesus could not use his power for destructive purposes to protect himself, a complete change in his appearance and the ability to suddenly disappear and reappear should have kept him safe from the Roman authorities and their local servants. It is also obvious that on the first day of his resurrection, Jesus had not yet regained his former physical characteristics, which is why he asked Magdalene not to touch him. On the same day and for the same reason, he suddenly disappears from the eyes of his followers, who finally recognize their Teacher by the way he prays and breaks bread. Later, the resurrected Jesus began to possess the necessary bodily features of the former one. From now on, he could be touched, one could "put the finger where the nails were" on his hands and in the ribs (from a spear). Jesus continued to eat bread, baked fish, and honeycomb with his disciples (Luke 24:42–43; John 20:27; 21:13).

The appearance of Jesus to the people.
A painting of A.A. Ivanov. 1837.

So that his disciples would understand that he was not a spirit, Jesus said to them, "Look at my hands and my feet. It is I myself! Touch me and see; a ghost does not have flesh and bones, as you see I have" (Luke 24:39). However, some biblical scholars do not rule out the possibility that those words were deliberately added by second-century copyists as a response to the docetism that bothered them. As is well known, the Docetians, supporters of this trend in early Christianity, claimed that the resurrected Jesus returned only as a "visible spirit." Unfortunately, it is not possible to refute or confirm this assumption. However, judging by the descriptions of various appearances of Christ, he was a visible spirit only on the first day of his resurrection—for example, when he appeared to Magdalene. Later, he regained his former material features, and that is how he appeared to his disciples.

How much can we trust the contradictory versions of the gospels about the resurrection of Jesus? The answer to this question is unequivocal—all these dissimilar narratives speak of an authentic event. If the authors of the gospels had decided to deceive their readers, they would never have made women the main witnesses to the disappearance of Jesus's body and the first to see the risen Christ. As a rule, the testimonies of women in the ancient world, especially in the Near East, were either not accepted or regarded as insufficient. It is not by chance that the disciples of Jesus did not believe their own women who came running from an empty cave. In the same way, the authors of the gospels, if they had wanted to deceive their audience, would never have reported on the new, unfamiliar appearance of the risen Jesus, an account that naturally lent itself to skepticism about whether it was Christ who had appeared or some other person pretending to be him. In short, in the gospel versions of the resurrection of Jesus, you can find a great deal that would never have been mentioned by people of that time who wanted to deceive others.

However, much more significant is the earliest New Testament testimony left by the apostle Paul two decades after the crucifixion. Paul claimed that Jesus appeared not only to his disciples and to his brother James, but "after that, he appeared to more than five hundred of the brothers and sisters at the same time, most of whom are still living, though some have fallen asleep" (1 Cor. 15:6).

When did these events occur? Unfortunately, we know no more about their dates than we do about the year and birthday of Jesus. According to Luke, Jesus was crucified in the thirty-third year of his life. If the most likely date of his birth is between 6 and 4 BCE, then the crucifixion and resurrection occurred between 27 and 29 CE. The crucifixion took place on the very eve of Passover, the holiday on the occasion of the Exodus from Egypt. Since the Jewish calendar is lunar, the date of this holiday varies from year to year. However, most often Passover is celebrated in April.

Fishing boat from the time of Jesus, found in the Kinneret area

How long did the resurrected Jesus appear to his disciples and followers? None of the gospels reports this. But the "Acts of the Apostles" gives the exact figure—forty days. This number is magical in the biblical tradition. At the age of forty, Moses fled Egypt, and forty years later returned there on a mission to save his people. For forty years, the Hebrew tribes wandered in the desert after the Exodus from Egypt. Forty thousand Israelites crossed the Jordan River to conquer Canaan. King David reigned forty years, and so did his wise son Solomon. For forty days, the prophet Elijah traveled to the mountain of the Lord—Horeb. Finally, Jesus himself, after being baptized by John, fasted in the wilderness for forty days and forty nights. Perhaps the author of Acts, the same Luke, found it necessary to use this magic number here. However, the actual period during which the resurrected Jesus appeared to his followers was likely to have been no less and possibly more than forty days. John, telling of Jesus's appearance to the seven disciples on the Sea of Galilee (Kinneret), mentioned that "as soon as Simon Peter heard him say, 'It is the Lord,' he wrapped his outer garment around him (for he had taken it off) and jumped into the water" (John 21:7). Even taking into account the warm climate in the Kinneret area, you can sit naked in a boat and then swim to the shore there not earlier than mid—May. Thus, the appearances of the risen Jesus would have taken place in April and May. At the same time, according to the Acts, Jesus ascended before Pentecost—the Jewish holiday of Shavuot, which is celebrated exactly seven weeks after Passover; therefore, the appearance of the risen Christ would have lasted less than 49 days.

Ascension

The narrative of the gospels about the Ascension of Jesus is even more problematic than the information about the resurrection. The two gospels, Matthew, and John, say nothing at all about the Ascension, as if this event did not happen. The third, from Mark, is limited by the very short phrase that "after the Lord Jesus had spoken to them (his disciples), he was taken up into heaven" (Mark 16:19). It couldn't be more concise. Only Luke says a little more: "When he had led them out to the vicinity of Bethany, he lifted up his hands and blessed them. While he was blessing them, he left them and was taken up into heaven" (Luke 24:50–51). Unfortunately, this important episode from the Gospel of Luke (24:51) was probably added much later; it is absent in Codex Sinaiticus. However, in his other work—in Acts—Luke reports something quite different, namely, that the Ascension of Jesus was not in Bethany (where he had raised Lazarus) but on "the hill called the Mount of Olives, a Sabbath day's walk from the city" (Acts. 1:12). The "Sabbath day's walk" usually meant to the city border, beyond which it was forbidden to go on Saturdays. Moreover, Luke introduces new characters to the scene of Jesus's Ascension:

> He was taken up before their very eyes, and a cloud hid him from their sight. They were looking intently up into the sky as he was going, when suddenly two men dressed in white stood beside them. "Men of Galilee," they said, "why do you stand here looking into the sky? This same Jesus, who has been taken from you into heaven, will come back in the same way you have seen him go into heaven." (Acts 9:11)

Why didn't Luke mention the two angels in his gospel, and why did he find it necessary to mention them in Acts?

What was most important to the disciples of Jesus before his Ascension? As good Jews, they were primarily concerned with the fate of their people. "Lord, are you at this time going to restore the kingdom to Israel?" they asked (Acts 1:6). This testified to the fact that even after the crucifixion and resurrection of Jesus, the disciples looked at their Teacher as the Jewish Messiah who, according to the Scriptures, was to restore the kingdom of David. Jesus did not consider it necessary to reveal the plans of his world, even to his disciples. And it is unlikely that his followers understood that the spread of the idea of monotheism by the Jews among other peoples was a more important task than the restoration of Judean statehood.

Why do the authors of the gospels either not mention the ascension or pay so little attention to it? This is probably not accidental. The Ascension for them is just one of the new abilities peculiar to the risen Jesus, who now goes to the world of our Creator, then returns again to humanity. Even Luke—the only author who narrates this event—makes it clear that Jesus did not leave this world forever, and he will return. This was the main hope of the early Christians, for if he ascended to the world of our Creator, then the souls of those who believe in him must also be there.

On the Second Coming of Christ

Will there be a Second Coming of Jesus? All New Testament sources give an affirmative answer to this question. Mark says the following about this: "At that time, people will see the Son of Man coming in clouds with great power and glory. And he will send his angels and gather his elect from the four winds, from the ends of the earth to the ends of the heavens" (Mark 13:26–27). However, the long-awaited coming of Jesus will also mean the end of the world: "But in those days, following that distress, the sun will be darkened and the moon will not give its light; the stars will fall from the sky, and the heavenly bodies will be shaken" (Mark 13:24–25).

The Gospel of Luke is also sure of the Second Coming of Jesus: "For the Son of Man in his day will be like the lightning, which flashes and lights up the sky from one end to the other" (Luke 17:24). However, according to Luke, a sufficient amount of time must pass before the next coming of Jesus. "I tell you, you will not see me again until you say, 'Blessed is he who comes in the name of the Lord'" (Luke 13:35). But no one knows, and most importantly, Jesus did not want to say. He warned people only to be ready for the hour of his second coming: "You also must be ready, because the Son of Man will come at an hour when you do not expect him" (Luke 12:40). Luke, referring to the words of Jesus, warns that the Second Coming of Christ can happen unexpectedly:

> Just as it was in the days of Noah, so also will it be in the days of the Son of Man. People were eating, drinking, marrying, and being given in marriage up to the day Noah entered the ark. Then the flood came and destroyed them all. It was the same in the days of Lot. People were eating and drinking, buying and selling, planting and building. But the day Lot left Sodom, fire and sulfur rained down from heaven and destroyed them all. It will be just like this on the day the Son of Man is revealed. (Luke 17:26–30)

But Luke, unlike Mark, quotes the words of Jesus that the anticipated apocalypse will be far from complete, and most importantly, will not afflict everyone: "I tell you, on that night two people will be in one bed; one will be taken and the other left. Two women will be grinding grain together; one will be taken and the other left" (Luke 17:34–36).

The same idea—about the selectivity of the apocalypse and the judgment of Jesus on people—is also carried out by Matthew: "For the Son of Man is going to come in his Father's glory with his angels, and then he will reward each person according to what they have done . . . All the nations will be gathered before him, and he will separate the people one from another as a shepherd separates the sheep from the goats" (Matthew 16:27; 25:32).

In all that concerns the Second Coming of Christ, the New Testament has one thing in common—the expectation of an imminent return of Jesus. In this regard, the last episode from the Gospel of John is very characteristic. There, Peter, whom Jesus entrusted to "shepherd his sheep," asks the Teacher about another disciple (John). "Jesus answered, "If I want him to remain alive until I return, what is that to you? You must follow me" (John 21: 22). The expectation of Christ's coming is also clearly seen in the Revelation of John the Evangelist: "Look, I am coming soon! My reward is with me, and I will give to each person according to what they have done" (Revelation 22:12). The same idea—the imminent return of Jesus—pervades all the epistles of the apostles. However, the early Christians did not have a clear idea of what would actually happen after the Second Coming of Jesus and his judgment. Many early Christian authors of the second and third centuries, such as Papias of Hierapolis, Irenaeus of Lyons, Apollinaris, Tertullian, and Justin, believed that the millennial kingdom of Christ awaited righteous people, and they imagined it in a material, earthly form. (*The Apostolic Fathers: Greek Texts and English Translations of their Writings.* Ed. by J. B. Lightfoot and J. R. Harmer, 2nd ed., Ada, Michigan: Baker Publication Group, 1992, p. 556).

But did his followers understand Jesus correctly? After all, he did not give any details. Moreover, as the Acts claim, he warned his disciples: "It is not for you to know the times or dates the Father has set by his own authority" (Acts 1:7). Two thousand years have passed since then; our world, full of evil, continues to exist, and Christ has not returned. This is the best proof that our earthly world has not yet fulfilled the purpose for which it was created. Those who were waiting for the imminent end of the world, the Second Coming of Jesus, and his judgment on people, clearly did not realize the nature of our material world as a purgatory and crucible of human souls. Nevertheless, the understanding that suffering purifies our souls and therefore is necessary and inevitable for their improvement is also present in the epistles of the apostles. "The Lord is not slow in keeping his promise, as some understand slowness. Instead, he is patient with you, not wanting anyone to perish, but everyone to come to repentance" (2 Peter 3:9).

Of course, our earthly world can perish suddenly, in a few days, but it can also survive safely for many millennia. The meaning and terms of the existence of our world are beyond the capabilities of human cognition.

Who wrote the gospels and when?

What do we know about the authors of the canonical gospels? Very little. Even worse, we cannot be sure that the authors of the four officially recognized gospels are the same as those by whose names we call them. After all, the Church fathers established the authorship of the gospels at least a century after they were written. For a century after their creation, these New Testament writings were anonymous. Most of the books of the Old Testament are anonymous works, and this gives them greater authority and significance. The authors of the gospels followed this biblical tradition.

The problem of authorship is directly related to fixing the time the New Testament sources were written. Easiest to determine was the time of writing the Gospel of Mark. Its content certainly indicates that the author knew about the Great Jewish Revolt against Rome (66–73 CE), but he did not yet know about the fall of Jerusalem and the destruction of the Temple (70 CE). It is therefore not surprising that many biblical scholars think the Gospel of Mark was written between 66 and 69, that is, forty years after the crucifixion of Jesus. It is clear that the authors of the other three gospels knew of the tragedy that befell Jerusalem and the Temple, so these New Testament books can be dated after 70 CE

Who was Mark, the author of the first gospel? He was neither a disciple nor a follower of Jesus during his lifetime. Mark could not have known or met Jesus, as in the likely year of Christ's crucifixion, he was a child living outside Judea, probably in Cyprus. John (Yochanan) Mark (his full name), belonged to the wealthy and educated part of the Jewish Diaspora. This explains his knowledge of Greek and Latin. At the same time, he received a thorough Jewish religious education, so he also knew Hebrew and Aramaic and was well versed in the Scriptures. He was a close relative of Joseph Barnabas, a Cypriot Jew and Levite by birth, who became one of the first apostles of Christianity among the Gentiles, and this relationship played a huge role in his life. Barnabas brought him to the first Christians, introduced him to the closest disciples of Christ (Peter and John) and acquainted him with the brother of Jesus (James) and later with the apostles Paul and Silas. For some time, Mark preached with Paul and Barnabas in Asia Minor. But Mark's relationship with Paul did not work out, and the apostles parted ways. Barnabas then took Mark with him to his native Cyprus, and Paul continued his preaching in Asia Minor and Greece, this time with Silas. Mark became closest to Peter. Each of them drew from the other what he lacked. Peter was an invaluable source of information for Mark about Jesus and his teaching. On the other hand, Mark's erudition, his knowledge of Greek and Latin and Scripture, were very useful to the "unschooled" Peter. Gradually, Peter became a member of Mark's family, and Mark became Peter's "beloved son," especially since Peter was old enough to be his father. One of the houses belonging to Mark's mother in Judea became the meeting place of the first Christian community. It is noteworthy that Peter, released from prison, hastened to go there (Acts 12:12). The last time the paths of Mark, Peter, and Paul crossed was in Rome in the early 60s. If Paul was waiting for the emperor's trial, what caused Peter to be there is unknown. But he probably also enjoyed the hospitality and assistance of Mark in Rome.

According to the few surviving memoirs of one of the earliest Church fathers, Papias of Hierapolis (60–130?), "Mark, when he became the translator of St. Peter, wrote down carefully, though not in the right order, everything that he remembered about the sayings and deeds of Jesus." Because Mark did not write for the Jewish but for the Greek and Roman environment, he was not concerned to prove that, by birth and descent, Jesus fully met the requirements of the biblical tradition for the Messiah. Not by chance, he ignored the version of the birth of Christ in Bethlehem from the descendants of King David. Nor did he mention the Immaculate Conception. Instead, he tried to explain Jewish traditions and customs, translating Hebrew and Aramaic words and expressions. It is in the Gospel of Mark that Jesus calls himself only the Son of Man and tries to hide in every possible way that he is the Messiah. The Gospel of Mark is not only the first but also the shortest of all the gospels. It is also, according to the unanimous opinion of experts in the field of ancient Greek, the simplest from a literary and linguistic point of view. The fact that Mark's main source of knowledge about Jesus was Peter is evidence of the truthfulness of his gospel. Of course, the four decades that passed since the preaching of Jesus, as well as Peter's lack of literacy, must have inevitably led to some distortions and shifts in chronology. It is also possible that Mark used other sources in Hebrew and Aramaic that have not been preserved.

Some Church fathers regard Mark as among the seventy followers whom Jesus sent in his name to preach in Judea. This, of course, would increase the authority and value of Mark's testimony about Jesus. There was also a tendency to identify Mark with a young man who "wearing nothing but a linen garment, was following Jesus" and witnessed the scene of Jesus's arrest in the Garden of Gethsemane. When the Roman soldiers seized this young man, "he fled naked, leaving his garment behind" (Mark 14:51–52). However, the historical record does not support this version.

The second gospel in terms of date of creation is probably the Gospel of Matthew. According to most biblical scholars, it was written in the '70s—at the latest,—the '80s. According to some linguists, this gospel was originally written in Greek and is not a translation from Aramaic or Hebrew. By Church tradition, its authorship is attributed to Matthew, a disciple of Jesus, and the fact that Matthew was a tax collector before joining Jesus implies at least a minimal degree of literacy—at least the ability to count and write. However, because he spoke Aramaic and

Hebrew, Matthew would not have known Greek well enough to write this gospel. In addition, most of the quotations from the Old Testament are borrowed not from the Tanakh (Hebrew Bible), but from the Septuagint (its Greek translation). But that's not all. The author of the Gospel of Matthew transferred almost all the text (more than 90 percent) from the Gospel of Mark to his book. If the evangelist Matthew had really been a disciple of Jesus, he would not have relied almost completely on Mark, who had never seen Christ.

The Church fathers (Irenaeus of Lyons, Eusebius of Caesarea) refer to the already mentioned Papias of Hierapolis, according to whom "Matthew composed his work originally in the Hebrew language and everyone translated it as best he could." It is very likely that Matthew, a disciple of Jesus, actually wrote down in Aramaic or Hebrew the sayings of his Teacher. These records, which were called in biblical science "source Q" were used later by the author of the Gospel of Matthew. In those days, such borrowing was not considered reprehensible and was generally accepted. The "source Q" created by the original Matthew has not come down to us, but it is likely that it gave the name Matthew to the entire gospel. Thus, in reality, the disciple Matthew can own only the authorship of the record that became one of the sources for this New Testament work. (This is similar to what happened in the case of Moses, who wrote only a small part of the Pentateuch, but the editors of the Bible, wanting to use his authority, extended his name to all five of the earliest books of the Old Testament.) If this assumption regarding Matthew is correct, then part of the Gospel of Matthew has an earlier origin than the writing of Mark. It is no coincidence that the Church tradition considers the Book of Matthew to be the very first gospel.

Who was the author of the Gospel of Matthew? We do not know his true name, but judging by his work, one can say with certainty that he, like Mark, came from among the educated Jews of the Diaspora, for whom Greek was the native language. At the same time, these exiled Jews had a good command of Aramaic and Hebrew and were knowledgeable in the Scriptures. Like Mark, the author of the Gospel of Matthew could not have met Jesus, as he belonged to the second generation of his followers. But unlike Mark, he wrote not for the Gentiles but for his fellow Jews, so he did not need to explain Judaic customs and the meaning of Hebrew and Aramaic words. The main task for this author was different: to prove that Jesus was the Messiah the Jewish people were awaiting. But for this, he needed to convince his audience that Jesus's birth and origin were consistent with the requirements of the biblical tradition, namely, that he descended from the line of King David and was born in Bethlehem. It is no accident that the Gospel of Matthew contains more quotations from the Old Testament than any other gospel, because the author tried to prove by means of Scripture that all the biblical predictions were fulfilled in Jesus. This gospel has one important advantage: in comparison with all other New Testament writings, it gives the most detailed account of Jesus's teaching. In particular, it contains the most complete version of the Sermon on the Mount. Unlike Mark, who focuses on events in the life of Jesus, Matthew concentrates on his teaching. If in the Gospel of Mark Christ acts more, in Matthew, he preaches more.

The third Gospel in order of its creation is the gospel of Luke. It appeared later than the New Testament Books of Mark and Matthew but certainly earlier than the Gospel of John. Many biblical scholars suggest that the '80s CE are the most likely time of creation for this work. Early Christian authors, such as Irenaeus of Lyons and Eusebius of Caesarea agree that its authorship belongs to Luke, who was an assistant and companion of the apostle Paul, a physician by profession. (Irenaeus, Against Heresies, III, 1, 1; Eusebius, Ecclesiastical History, VI, 25). Modern biblical studies also have no reason to doubt that Luke wrote this gospel. Among the authors of the New Testament, Luke was the only one who was not a Jew by birth. However, he later became one by conviction. From what little we know, Luke was born in Antioch. According to one version, he was a Greek; according to another, a Syrian; a third has him as a Macedonian. In any event, the most significant fact about him is that in his cultural orientation, upbringing, and education, he belonged to the Hellenistic environment. Being highly educated, inquisitive, and of keen intelligence, he could not be satisfied with the Greco-Roman and Near Eastern pagan cults. In search of the true God, he rejects the idolatry of Hellenistic culture and draws closer to Judaism. In those days, Luke's act was typical of many educated Greeks, Romans, and Syrians: they were all attracted to Jewish monotheism. We do not know whether Luke officially became a Jew after being circumcised or whether he remained only a Judaized Hellene, of which there were many at that time. Called "God-fearers" or "God-worshippers," they studied Judaic customs and laws, led a Jewish way of life, and participated in services in synagogues. The need for circumcision kept many men from fully converting to Judaism.

Luke first met the followers of Jesus in the synagogues of Antioch and immediately joined them. Most of all, he became close to Paul, Barnabas, and Silas, who believed that in order to become a Christian, it was not necessary to be a Jew and observe Judaic laws and customs. But Paul went the furthest. In his opinion, after the resurrection of Jesus, only universal values—God, Scripture, and morality—should be taken from Judaism, and national traditions and customs should be left aside. Luke warmly embraced this idea and became Paul's associate and companion on his missionary trips. They visited Greece and Macedonia together, and Luke accompanied Paul when he was sent to the emperor's court in Rome. Like Mark and Matthew, Luke represented the second generation of Jesus's followers, who had never seen him and so wrote their books from the memories and records of eyewitnesses. We do not know all the sources that were in Luke's possession, but two of them are known with certainty: the Gospel of Mark, from which he borrowed a good half of the text and the previously mentioned source "Q," first used by Matthew. Did he know about the Gospel of Matthew? Probably yes, but he took very little from it.

Unlike Mark, who addressed the Gentiles, and Matthew, who dedicated his work to the Jews, Luke wrote for everyone, but most of all for the new Christians from among the Gentiles. That is why Luke, unlike Matthew, does not emphasize the messianic aspirations of the Jews and does not try to prove that Jesus is the Messiah that the Jewish people have been waiting for. Jesus in the Gospel of Luke is the Savior of all people, not just the Jews, and he belongs to all nations, not just the Judeans. This gospel contains much information that is not found in any other New Testament writing. For example, only here can you find information about the family of John the Baptist and the relationship of Jesus and John. The Gospel of Luke surpasses not only the rest of the gospels but also all the New Testament writings combined, both in terms of volume and in terms of art and language. Moreover, Luke's contribution to the creation of the New Testament is not limited to the gospel bearing his name; he is the author of another New Testament book—The Acts of the Holy Apostles. Both works share linguistic characteristics and have a similar literary style.

Church tradition includes Luke among the seventy followers of Jesus whom he sent to preach in Judea. According to the same tradition, Luke was an unnamed companion of Cleopas, who was on the way from Jerusalem to the village of Emmaus when they met Jesus on the first day of his resurrection. Both of these claims are intended to increase the authority of the Gospel of Luke as a work written by one of Jesus's disciples and a witness to his resurrection, but neither has anything to do with reality. In the year of Jesus's crucifixion, Luke was at best only just born in Antioch, far beyond the borders of Judea.

Despite their differences from each other, the Gospels of Mark, Matthew, and Luke contain many common or parallel episodes. This is because the main Hebrew and Aramaic sources used to write them were common and because the later gospels—Matthew and Luke—borrowed much of their text from the Book of Mark. It is no coincidence that these three writings are called synoptic ("seeing all together"—in Greek), since they either repeat or complement each other. Nothing like this can be said about the fourth work—the Gospel of John. It is certainly the last of the gospels, written about 95–100 CE in Asia Minor (perhaps Ephesus), seventy years or so after the crucifixion. Church tradition attributes the authorship of this gospel to Jesus's beloved disciple, John Zebedee. Five New Testament writings: the Gospel of John, "Revelation", and three apostolic epistles were written by this same author, to whom the Church awarded an honorary name—John the Evangelist. But could an illiterate fisherman from Galilee, John Zebedee, create five works of the New Testament, and in good Greek? After all, as the Acts recognize, John was considered an "unschooled, ordinary man" (Acts. 4:13). John Zebedee himself, who spoke Hebrew and Aramaic, was at best able to read the Tanakh (Hebrew Bible). He could not have known either the Greek language or even Greek philosophy because he lived in a simple, purely Jewish environment and did not receive any education, especially Greek. How could he have written or even dictated the phrase with which the Gospel of John begins: "In the beginning was the Word, and the Word was with God, and the Word was God" (John 1:1). After all, the author of this phrase meant the Logos and should have a firm grasp of ancient Greek philosophy. In addition, we must not forget that by the time of the writing of this gospel, John Zebedee would have reached almost a hundred years of age! There is no doubt that John the Evangelist, who wrote five New Testament works, has nothing to do with the disciple of Jesus—John Zebedee.

So who was the author of the fourth gospel, called John the Evangelist? He, like Mark and Matthew, was also an educated Jew from the Diaspora who probably belonged not to the second but the third generation of followers of Jesus. Of course, he could not have known Jesus; at the time Christ finished his earthly journey, John the Evangelist had not yet begun his own. Perhaps the true author of the fourth gospel knew the elderly John Zebedee and had even heard him recount his memories, and used the name of such a respected apostle to give his works as much authority and significance as possible. In those distant times, authors cared more for the fate of their creations than the fame of their own names, so they often attributed authorship of their books to people well known and revered. John the Evangelist presented his gospel in such a way as to convince the reader that its author was John Zebedee—the beloved disciple of Christ. John's longevity and closeness to Jesus were the main factors in choosing his name for all five New Testament writings. There is almost complete consensus in modern biblical studies that John Zebedee could not have been the author of the Gospel of John. In the search for the real author, many researchers point to the "elder John," the presbyter of the Christian community in Ephesus, as one of the most likely creators of this work. However, the true author of the fourth gospel did not necessarily have to have the same name as John Zebedee and to live in Ephesus. It should be remembered that the Church tradition granting authorship to John Zebedee is based primarily on the claims of Irenaeus of Lyons (130–200 CE), who in turn refers to the words of the bishop of Smyrna (now Turkish Izmir) Polycarp (ca. 85–167 CE). It was Polycarp who pointed to John Zebedee as the author of the gospel and claimed that he himself was a disciple of this (centenarian!) apostle. By the way, the same Polycarp wrote three "pastoral" epistles (the 1st and 2nd) to Timothy and Titus but presented them as letters of the apostle Paul.

Serious doubt about the authorship of the two gospels—Matthew and John—was reflected in the decision of the Catholic Church's Second Vatican Council (1962–65) not to insist that Jesus's disciples Matthew and John were their authors but instead to use another term—"holy authors."

The Gospel of John is not written for the Gentiles, as was Mark, or for the Jews, as was Matthew, or for all, as was the Gospel of Luke. The fourth gospel was created exclusively for new Christians from the Hellenes. If Mark describes the events in the life of Jesus, Matthew expounds the teachings of Christ, and Luke creates the image of the Savior of all people, then John philosophically interprets the nature of Jesus and his mission. The author uses the categories of ancient Greek philosophy to be understood by the Greeks. It is no coincidence that many people call the work of John a "spiritual" gospel. John's Christ is not the Son of Man, as in the Gospel of Mark, nor the Jewish Messiah, as in the Gospel of Matthew, nor even the Savior of the human race, as in the Gospel of Luke. In the Gospel of John, he is the Son of God. Only in this gospel are words such as "for I have come down from heaven" (John 6:38), "I am the light of the world" (John 8:12), "I and the Father are one" (John 10:30) put into the mouth of Jesus. It is here that Jesus calls himself God and says: "Before Abraham was born, I am" (John 8:58). This is completely contrary to the Synoptic Gospels, according to which Jesus hid in every possible way that he is the Messiah. But the Messiah is not God or the Son of God but only a messenger of the Lord, an intermediary between him and humanity. The Jesus of John is no longer the Jesus of Nazareth in Judea but the Christ from the icon in the Christian Church. This is no longer the Savior of the "lost sheep of Israel" but the Son of God who sits on the throne and judges the living and the dead. As a matter of fact, the Gospel of John is both the constitution and the program of the early Christian Church, which finally breaks with Judaism and formulates the essence of the new religion.

If the Synoptic Gospels tell about the events and preaching of Jesus mainly in Galilee, then the book of John tells about Christ's stay in Judea itself, in particular Jerusalem. In the Gospel of John, unlike Matthew and Luke, there are almost no parables. In John, Jesus is a pronounced apocalyptic and predicts a very rapid end of the world that is not found in the Synoptic Gospels. Only in the Gospel of John is there an underlying criticism of the heretics—the Gnostics, the Docetians, and the Ebionites—with whom the early Christian Church struggled. This fact alone indicates that the Gospel of John was not created until the end of the first century, when these heresies actually appeared.

It must be admitted that in historical terms, the Synoptic Gospels are much more reliable than the writing of John. However, the last gospel has its own merits: It gives us details of the life of Jesus that are not found in any other New Testament writings. More than 90 percent of its text is unique and has no analogies or parallels in the New Testament. For example, only here do we find the story of the resurrection of Lazarus, the conversation with the Samaritan woman, and the talks with the Pharisee Nicodemus. The author of this gospel used sources that were unknown or inaccessible to Mark, Matthew, and Luke. It is very possible they were the manuscripts of such educated Pharisees and scribes as Nicodemus, who openly sympathized with Jesus. Unlike the illiterate disciples of Christ, these people had sufficient knowledge to write down his sayings and leave a memory of him and his mission. But the secret followers of Jesus from the Pharisees and scribes lived, as a rule, not in the provincial Galilee, but in the center of the country—in Judea and Jerusalem. This may explain the fact that the Gospel of John tells mainly about Jesus' sojourn in Judea and Jerusalem.

Although the sources for all the gospels were manuscripts in Hebrew and Aramaic, the gospels themselves, including the Book of Matthew, were written in Koine Greek—the common form of ancient Greek spoken in Eastern Mediterranean countries in the Hellenistic and Roman periods. The books of Mark and John are written at the simplest level of Koine and the gospel of Matthew at a higher level. The richest and most elegant language, although colloquial, was found in the works of Luke. As for the Hebrew manuscripts that served as sources for writing the gospels, none of them have come down to us. Either they did not survive the trials of centuries, or they were deliberately not preserved because of inconsistency with the dogmas of the Church.

The evaluation of the gospels from the point of view of historical authenticity puts the work of Mark in the first place. Despite the fact that it is the shortest and was written in the simplest Greek language, it is the earliest, and most importantly, the truest evidence of events in Judea at that time. In addition, there is no doubt about Mark's authorship and the sources of his knowledge of Jesus. The second place in reliability belongs to the Gospel of Matthew. It is followed by the Books of Luke and John, respectively. Of course, none of these gospels is a documentary historical record. All of them are literary works of varying artistic merit and express the points of view of their authors, which do not always coincide with each other. Each of them contains the traces of texts from earlier manuscripts that have not come down to us.

The authors of the gospels have very different attitudes to the laws and practices of Judaism. So, Mark and Matthew, basically, adhere to the opinion of the apostle Peter, according to which, faith in Christ does not cancel the need for Jews to observe all the rites, traditions, and customs of Judaism. At the same time, Luke and John reflect the point of view of Paul, who believed that faith in Christ alone exempts not only Gentiles but also Jews themselves from the obligation to comply with Judaic laws.

In the history of the early Church of the second century, there are known attempts to make only one of the four gospels the main canonical work. For example, the Jewish Christians, including the Ebionites, considered only the Gospel of Matthew to be the most "correct" since it did not abolish the laws of Judaism for believers in Christ. Some Christian communities, who saw Jesus primarily as the Son of Man, recognized only the Gospel of Mark. Finally, there were numerous groups of Gnostic

Christians. Some of them, in particular the supporters of Marcion, adhered to the Gospel of Luke, while others—the followers of Valentine—accepted only the Gospel of John.

Who distorted the gospels and why?

The original texts of the canonical gospels have not reached us. Their earliest complete copies that are known to us date only to the fourth century. These are the so-called Codex Sinaiticus and Codex Vaticanus. However, in the first three centuries since the creation of the gospels, their texts have undergone significant changes. In contrast to the Middle Ages, when the copying of New Testament writings took place in monasteries by the most literate and skilled monks and under strict control, the situation in the 2nd to 3rd centuries was completely different. The first copyists were random individuals, not always sufficiently literate and often inexperienced, and they made many mistakes. But the deeper issue was that the official canon had not yet been formed, and those who were engaged in copying therefore considered themselves entitled to "improve" the text of the gospels in accordance with their own views or the opinions prevailing in their Christian communities. This resulted in deliberate distortions and additions. The fathers of the Church in the second and third centuries repeatedly complained about the insolence and excess of the copyists who allowed themselves to edit the New Testament works. In this regard, it is remarkable to read the complaint of Origen, one of the fathers of the early Church (3rd century): "The differences between the manuscripts have become significant. This is due both to the carelessness and impudence of the scribes. They either do not check what they copy, or add and subtract what they please" (Bruce M. Metzger, "Explicit References in the Works of Origen to Variant Readings in New Testament Manuscripts," in *Biblical and Patristic Studies in Memory of Robert Pierce Casey*, ed. J. Neville Birdsall and Robert W. Thomson, Freiburg: Herder, 1968, pp. 78–9).

As already mentioned, B. Ehrman quotes Dionysius, bishop of Corinth (2nd century), who also drew attention to the fact that copyists distort the gospels, making inserts in them at their own discretion: "When my brothers in Christ suggested that I write them epistles, I agreed.—However, the disciples of Satan (copyists) filled them with tares, removing one and adding another, woe be unto them. It is not surprising that they also forged the Scriptures." Ehrman emphasizes that not only heretics but also copyists from among Orthodox Christians were engaged in distorting the gospels. (Bart D. Ehrman, *The Orthodox Corruption of Scripture: The Effects of Early Christological Controversies on the Text of the New Testament*, New York: Oxford University Press, 1993). In his opinion, these distortions of the New Testament writings took on such threatening proportions that in their later works, the authors themselves were forced to introduce warnings to dishonest copyists. As an example, he points to Revelation 22:18–1, where John the Evangelist threatens terrible punishments to anyone who distorts his work (Rev.).

References to the distortion of the original texts of the gospels came not only from leaders of Christian communities but also from opponents of Christianity, in particular the famous Roman pagan writer Celsus. He blamed Christian copyists for outright falsification of evangelical texts: "They change the original text of the gospels three or four times, many times, and alter it until they are able to evade all objections" (Henry Chadwick, *Origen's "Contra Celsum,"* Cambridge: The University Press, 1953, 2.27). Text distortions can be divided into two main categories: accidental and intentional. Accidental errors, which include numerous typos and omissions of words and even whole phrases, were involuntary in nature and are explained by the professional unpreparedness of the first copyists. Much more serious were the deliberate changes in the New Testament works. But what exactly did the copyists change? First of all, they tried to make it so that supporters of early Christian heresies could not refer to the gospels to justify their views. For example, with the Gnostics in mind, the copyists made additions to the texts that emphasized that God, the Father of Jesus and the God of the Jews, the Creator of our world, are one and the same Lord. At that time, this was very important, because the Gnostics claimed that there were at least two gods: the main one who does only good (he is also the God-Father of Christ), and the second one, a lower-level deity, who created our evil world, who is actually the God of wrath and revenge from the Old Testament.

The second most important heresy was that of the Ebionites and those who saw in Jesus only a man, denying his divinity. In biblical studies, such views are called "adoptionist" (from the word *adoption*), since their supporters believed that God adopted Jesus and made him the Messiah only at the baptism of John the Baptist. In an attempt to knock the ground out from under the feet of the adoptionists, copyists made inserts that claimed that Jesus was not only the Son of Man but also the Son of God and therefore had both human and divine nature. In the same way, the copyists tried to counteract the supporters of docetism, who believed that the resurrected Jesus was only a visible spirit. In this case, the copyists tried to emphasize in the gospels that the risen Christ could be touched and it was possible even to put one's fingers in his wounds; moreover, he ate food with everyone else. Such changes in the texts served the purpose of combating heretical teachings, but they certainly distorted the words of the authors of the gospels.

Another theological problem of the time was the dogma of the Immaculate Conception. The adoptionists believed that Jesus was born just like any other person. And today we know that they had every reason to think so. The Codex Sinaiticus (4th century) from Saint Catherine's monastery in Sinai has the oldest known text of the Gospel of Matthew, which says of the birth of Jesus: "Jacob begat Joseph; Joseph, to whom the virgin Mary was betrothed, begat Jesus, called Christ." Thus, in the original version, the father of Jesus was Joseph. However, the copyists changed the text, and in the current canon, it looks completely different: "Jacob the father of Joseph, the husband of Mary, and Mary was the mother of Jesus who is called the Messiah" (Matthew 1:16). Here, Joseph is no longer the father of Christ, although he is still the husband of Mary.

Other reasons prompted copyists to change the texts of the gospels. In trying to show the loyalty of Christians to Rome, the copyists removed all the anti-Roman episodes, of which there must have been many in the original texts. After all, Jesus and his disciples lived and preached mostly in Galilee, the epicenter of Jewish resistance to Rome. If not Jesus himself, then at least his disciples could not be silent about the Roman occupants and those who fought against them. Moreover, among the disciples of Christ was the uncompromising fighter for the freedom of Judea, Simon Cananeus ("the Zealot"). The absence of any mention of the Romans and their repressions is as strange and unnatural as would, for example, complete silence about the Germans and Germany in World War II. However, the copyists not only threw out all the anti-Roman statements, they also changed the evangelical texts in such a way as to remove responsibility from the Roman authorities for the execution of Jesus. To do this, they had to profoundly revise the scenes of the arrest and interrogation of Jesus, as a result of which the blame for the crucifixion was placed on the Jews. For the same reason, they also made anti-Jewish additions that often openly contradicted the meaning and spirit of the gospels. The Gospel of John suffered most of all from anti-Jewish inserts. Here, as in no other New Testament work, the copyists demonstrated a complete ignorance of the geography, culture, and religious traditions of Judea. Moreover, in order to demonize the Jews, they have inserted into original text additions that go against the very context of the gospel itself. An example is this accusation against the Jews blatantly put into the mouth of Jesus: "You belong to your father, the devil, and you want to carry out your father's desires. He was a murderer from the beginning, not holding to the truth, for there is no truth in him. When he lies, he speaks his native language, for he is a liar and the father of lies . . . The reason you do not hear is that you do not belong to God" (John 8:44, 47). This addition, which has nothing to do with either Christ or the author of the work, John the Evangelist, clearly does not fit the text of the gospel, where Jesus emphasizes just the opposite, that "for salvation is from the Jews" (John 4:22). Such an insertion, and there are many of them in the Gospel of John, contradicts the Synoptic Gospels, according to which Jesus is the son of the Jewish people and came to our world primarily to save his people. If in the Synoptic Gospels only the Pharisees and Sadducees are the main opponents of Jesus, the first copyists of the Gospel of John managed to turn all the Jews into enemies of Christ.

We have reason to believe that the original texts of the canonical gospels did not contain any anti-Jewish claims; moreover, there was not even a hint of blame for the crucifixion of Christ on the Jews. Anti-Jewish additions and insertions were made later, in the first half of the second century. This was done by the first copyists of the gospels, usually Hellenes, who had a traditional hostility to their more successful rivals, the Jews. The copyists tried to distort the original texts in such a way as to tear the preaching of Christ out of the mainstream of Judaism and create an impression of alienation between Jesus and his people. To the same end, they exaggerated both the intensity of Jesus's controversy with the Pharisees and the differences in their views. Perhaps this practice of making anti-Jewish additions to the gospels gained support from the heads of Christian communities, especially after the former pagans prevailed in numbers over the Jews (from the 2nd century), and the leadership passed to the Gentiles.

What language did Christ speak?

In May 2014, Pope Francis made an official visit to the Holy Land. While speaking with Prime Minister Benjamin Netanyahu in Jerusalem, the pontiff unwittingly entered into a controversy with him about the language of Christ. In response to the Israeli Prime Minister's words that "Jesus lived just in this country and spoke Hebrew," Francis said that Christ spoke Aramaic. "Yes, he spoke Aramaic," Netanyahu acknowledged, "but he also knew Hebrew." This brief diplomatic dispute reminded everyone of the serious scientific debate that has unfolded in recent decades about the language of Jesus. What language did the Son of Man actually speak and preach?

Until the mid-20th century, the belief prevailed in historical science and biblical studies that in the period of the Second Temple (5th century BCE–70 CE), the Jews switched from Hebrew to Aramaic. The beginning of this transition was the Babylonian Captivity, when for half a century many Jews found themselves in the Aramaic cultural environment in Mesopotamia. After returning to their homeland, Judea, their spiritual revival was led by the teacher of the law Ezra and the Persian governor Nehemiah, who also grew up in Babylonia and spoke Aramaic. To us reached Nehemiah's complaint that the former Babylonian captives no longer speak Hebrew (Neh. 13:23–24). In order to emphasize the difference between the Jews and the Samaritans, Ezra deliberately abandoned the old Hebrew script of the time of David and Solomon in favor of the square Aramaic script, which he had adopted in Babylonia. However, that the Jews voluntarily switched to Aramaic should not have been surprising because Aramaic was in fact never foreign to the Jews. It must not be forgotten that Hebrew and Aramaic are closely related, and both belong to the same Northwest Semitic language group. Moreover, the Bible calls the descendants of Nahor, the brother of the patriarch Abraham, Arameans, making it clear that this people is related to the Hebrews (Genesis 22:21). The Arameans have always been the closest neighbors, allies, tributaries, and often dangerous enemies of the Israelites and Judahites.

In the 12th to 11th century BCE, Aramaic tribes (of the same West Semitic origin as the Jews) spread throughout the Near East, and with them spread their language, which became the lingua franca of that time. Aramaic was spoken in Assyria and Babylonia, in Syria and Phoenicia. This language was brought to Judea by Babylonian captives, and until recently, it was believed that from the 5th century BCE, Aramaic replaced Hebrew. The fact that the latest parts of the Old Testament, such as the Books of Ezra and Daniel, were written in Aramaic was seen as evidence that this language had already become dominant in Judea. The presence of a large number of Aramaic words in the gospels also seemed to confirm that.

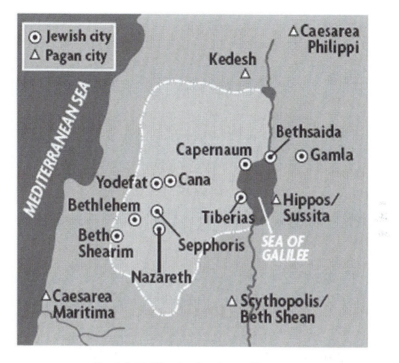

Jewish Galilee in the time of Jesus.

However, since the mid-20th century, numerous archaeological discoveries have forced most historians to radically change their minds about the linguistic situation in Judea during the Second Temple period. The first serious blow to the belief of the dominance of the Aramaic language at this time was the discovery of the Dead Sea Scrolls, found in the Qumran caves. Almost all of them were written not in Aramaic but in Hebrew. But why write in a language that is already out of use? Perhaps tradition required that religious texts be written only in the language of the Bible. But the inscriptions on ceramics, coins, and stones were made exclusively in Hebrew, and they cannot be explained by religious tradition. Finally, the discovery of new inscriptions in Masada and the letters of Bar Kokhba, the leader of the second Jewish revolt against Rome in 132–135 CE, once and for all convinced most historians that Hebrew was not replaced by Aramaic and remained spoken throughout the Second Temple period. In this regard, it is appropriate to recall the claim of the second-century father of the Church, Papias of Hierapolis, that the Gospel of Matthew was originally written in Hebrew and not in Aramaic or Koine Greek. In addition, a study of the New Testament writings, in particular the same gospels, showed that the number of Hebrew words in them is actually no less than the Aramaic ones. And the New Testament book Acts of the Holy Apostles twice recalls that the apostle Paul addressed the crowd of his fellow Jews in Jerusalem in Hebrew, and not in Aramaic (Acts. 21:40; 22:2). According to the same book, the apostle Paul, on his way to Damascus, heard the voice of Christ addressing him in Hebrew and not in Aramaic (Acts 26:14). In this case, the author of the Acts, Luke, can be fully trusted because he knew the apostle Paul very well and was his disciple and friend, and later his companion on his last journey to Rome.

Mona Lisa of Galilee. Mosaic portrait from Sepphoris, 3rd century CE.

Moreover, could the return of the Babylonian captives to Judea have completely change the linguistic situation in the country? After all, the Babylonian exile affected only a small part of the Judahite population: the nobility, the royal court, priests, scribes, soldiers, and the most skilled artisans went into captivity. Almost all the peasants and residents of many cities, who made up the absolute majority of the population, remained in their former places and continued to speak Hebrew. The return of the Babylonian captives, who had switched to Aramaic, would have only Arameanized the Hebrew language and added many Aramaic words and expressions to it, which in fact happened. The language of worship was still Hebrew, and so it was not likely to disappear.

The Hebrew language of the time of Jesus is best preserved in the Mishnah—the first book that records the interpretation of the Oral Law (Oral Torah). If the language of the era of David and Solomon (10th century BCE), as well as the period of the existence of the kingdoms of Israel (928–722 BCE) and Judah (928–587 BCE) is called Biblical Hebrew, then the language of the inhabitants of Judea of the last two centuries BCE and the first centuries CE is defined as Mishnaic Hebrew. Today we can give a clear and unambiguous answer to the question about the language of Christ: the Son of Man spoke and preached in Mishnaic Hebrew, that is, an Arameanized Hebrew. It is noteworthy that of all the biblical and post-biblical books, it was the Mishnah that served as the main source for the revival of Hebrew in modern times, since its vocabulary turned out to be the richest. As a result, the closest thing to the language of Christ was not the Biblical Hebrew of the time of David and Solomon but the revived Hebrew of the modern State of Israel.

The influence of Aramaic on Hebrew can be traced not only to those Jews who lived in Babylonia but also through contacts with the Arameans themselves, who inhabited the northeastern outskirts of Palestine. The people of the northernmost part of the country, Galilee, where Jesus actually grew up, were subjected to the greatest Arameanization. Their speech was full of Aramaic words and expressions, so the residents of Jerusalem unmistakably could identify the natives of Galilee (Acts. 2:7). As a Galilean, Jesus must have had a good command of the Aramaic language, and most likely, it was in this language that he spoke to a Syrophoenician (Canaanite) woman from the region of Tyre when she asked him to heal her daughter of demon possession.

It is much more difficult to judge whether Jesus knew Greek, and if so, to what extent. Unlike their fellows in the Diaspora, Jews in Judea itself generally did not know Greek. According to Josephus, it was difficult to find a Jew in Judea at that time who could speak Greek. Galilee was a Jewish-dominated area, and the Hellenistic cities where Greek and Aramaic were spoken were only small patches in the solid mass of the Judean population. Although Jesus's native Nazareth was only three miles from the famous Hellenistic city of Sepphoris, the influence of Greek culture and language was felt only within its city walls. Relations between Jews and Hellenes were strained. The Jews were burdened by the proximity of idolaters, and the Hellenes, in turn, feeling the support of the Roman army, defiantly ignored the traditions and customs of Judea, although they lived on its land.

The Jews tried not to visit the cities of the pagans, and where they had to live with them—for example, in Caesarea—there were permanent conflicts. It is no coincidence that the Hellenistic Sepphoris is never mentioned in any of the gospels, although it was located far closer to Nazareth than Capernaum, Bethsaida, or Cana. Neither Jesus nor his disciples preached among the Hellenistic pagans. We have every reason to believe that the Son of Man and his disciples did not know Greek. However, some biblical scholars, trying to find confirmation that Jesus did know Greek, refer to those episodes from the gospels where Christ speaks with Pontius Pilate or with a Roman centurion who asked to heal his servant. Of course, almost no one knew Latin in Judea, so both the Romans and the Jews resorted to the help of interpreters to communicate with each other. The Jews who lived in Judea did not understand Greek, although it was still more common than Latin. The gospel episodes can neither confirm nor deny that Jesus spoke Greek. After all, the real authors of the gospels were neither companions nor contemporaries of Christ, and their works are not documentary chronicles but literary works created on the basis of authentic events. Even the authors of the gospels did not know if anyone had translated the conversation between Jesus and Pilate. If Pilate really had spoken to Jesus, then only a witness to this conversation, probably an interpreter, could tell about it. As for Jesus's communication with the Roman centurion, it could also have been in Aramaic, since the majority of the Roman garrison in Judea consisted of Syrians of Aramaic origin. There is also an opinion that if Jesus at the moment of death on the cross, according to the Gospel of Mark, called to the Father in Aramaic, then he also spoke and preached in this language (Mark 15:34). However, in the Gospel of Matthew, the same phrase is given in Mishnaic Hebrew, and in Luke, there are completely different words, even in the Greek translation

(Matthew 27:46; Luke 23:46). John gives a new, third version of Jesus's dying words, again in Greek (John 19:30). All this once again confirms that the authors of the gospels were not eyewitnesses to the described events; therefore, adhering to different points of view and using different sources, they depicted the same scenes far differently from one another.

The amphitheater in Sepphoris.

PART THREE

First Christians

JUDEA IN THE TIMES of Jesus lived by messianic aspirations; the Jewish people awaited the coming of the Messiah, who was to free the country of Roman pagans and restore the kingdom of David. In this spiritually tense situation, there appeared many wandering preachers who gathered around themselves disciples and followers. Some confined themselves strictly to peaceful preaching and called for righteousness and asceticism. Others insisted on decisively fighting against the Roman invaders and their appointed authorities. Of the peaceful preachers, the most well known was John the Baptist, and of the militant, the most prominent was Judas of Galilee. However, a common element was typical to the disciples and followers of all these leaders: they dissipated and disappeared without a trace as soon as their spiritual mentor died or, most often, perished.

Nothing of the sort happened with the followers of Jesus. Even after his crucifixion, they did not scatter but preserved their organizational structure, at the head of which were the disciples, chosen by the Teacher himself. Leadership passed on to Peter, the oldest and most authoritative disciple, to whom Christ gave the duty of "taking care of his sheep." Admittedly, the people who remained loyal to Jesus were few and numbered no more than 120 (Acts 1:16). All or most of them were from Galilee. Only after Jesus's execution did they move to Jerusalem, where they were to wait for the Counselor, the Holy Spirit, who Christ promised to send (John 14:16–17,26). Jesus's mother, along with his brothers, moved there too, and the Temple of Jerusalem became the primary place of prayer and gathering for Christ's followers. To the city's residents, these people were known as "Nazarenes"—referring to the small town of Nazareth, where Jesus came from. However, those who took the oath to lead a semi-monastic way of life, to not cut their hair or drink wine, and to not touch the dead, were called Nazarenes as well. Thus the name Nazarene also connoted for most people a modest, almost ascetic way of life.

The Nazarenes

The main difference between the Nazarenes—the first Christians—and the other forms of Judaism was the belief in Jesus as the Jewish Messiah (Christ). In this way, the Nazarenes departed from biblical tradition, according to which the Messiah was not to suffer at the hands of the enemies of the Jewish people but to defeat those enemies and "to restore the kingdom to Israel" (Acts 1:6). The Nazarenes put emphasis on Jesus's resurrection, which in itself testified to them to the messianic nature of their Teacher. It was precisely because of this belief that they, unlike the Pharisees and Sadducees, were apocalyptics, awaiting the forthcoming end of the world, as well as the Second Coming of Christ and his judgment over the people.

The second distinctive trait of the Nazarenes was their liberal attitude to the laws of the Oral Torah. In this, they completely adhered to Jesus's teaching, who recognized the Oral Torah but deemed its laws to be of human creation, not of God's. However, it is unlikely that the Nazarenes departed from Judaism over this issue; after all, the Sadducees—priests of the Temple of Jerusalem—did not recognize the Oral Torah at all, believing it to be the invention of the Pharisees. In all else, the Nazarenes did not differ in any way from the other trends of Judaism. Moreover, this group was converging with the Essenes in a number of ways. Both groups were united by a contemptuous attitude to wealth and by the sharing of common property. The Nazarenes, like the Essenes, shared all the means available to them in accordance with the needs of their communities' members. This is what Acts tells us of the Nazarenes' views on property:

> All the believers were together and had everything in common. They sold property and possessions to give to anyone who had need . . . All the believers were one in heart and mind. No one claimed that any of their possessions was their own, but they shared everything

they had . . . there were no needy persons among them. For from time to time those who owned land or houses sold them, brought the money from the sales and put it at the apostles' feet, and it was distributed to anyone who had need. (Acts 2:44–45; 4:32,34–35)

It is important to note that neither Jesus nor John the Baptist demanded that the people sacrifice their property for the common good; however, Jesus did expect this of all who wanted to join his circle of closest disciples.

The Nazarenes shared other beliefs with the Essenes. They believed in the immortality of the soul, as well as reward and retribution in the afterlife for what was done in the material world; they similarly called for obedience to the authorities, believing that any power came from God. However, most of what united the Nazarenes with the Essenes— like faith in predestination and a special attitude to oaths—came from Jesus. Like the Essenes, Jesus urged people to not swear at all and to not take anything with them when on the road (Mark 6:8–10). The closeness between the Nazarenes and the Essenes serves as evidence that Jesus, like John the Baptist, not only knew the Essenes well but likely learned many of their ideas and views when living among them in his adolescence or youth.

New disciple

One of the very first steps the Nazarenes took was the election of a new disciple, the 12th disciple, instead of Judas Iscariot. This spoke of the desire of the first Christians to be the executors of the will of Jesus. As Christ intended, the number of his disciples was to correspond to the twelve Hebrew tribes and represent a symbolic link with Israelite history and biblical tradition. The story of the choice of a new disciple indirectly confirms the fact that the disciples of Jesus did not come to their Teacher by chance: they had previously formed the closest circle of John the Baptist and joined Jesus at the behest of John himself, when he was captured by the servants of Herod Antipas. The new disciple was chosen from among those who had gone all the way with the Teacher, from the baptism of John to the Ascension of Christ. The candidates also had to have been witnesses of the resurrection of Jesus (Acts 1:21–22). As it turned out, there were only two who met these conditions: Joseph, called Barsabbas (also known as Justus), and Matthias. "Then they cast lots, and the lot fell to Matthias; so he was added to the eleven apostles" (Acts 1:26).

"Confusion of the languages"

Acts tells of the "confusion of tongues" when the followers of Jesus suddenly spoke in languages that they did not know before. This happened on Pentecost (Shavuot), a Jewish holiday dedicated to receiving the Torah on Mount Sinai. It was then that the disciples of Jesus sat down for the first time to a festive meal without their Teacher. "Suddenly a sound like the blowing of a violent wind came from heaven and filled the whole house where they were sitting. They saw what seemed to be tongues of fire that separated and came to rest on each of them. All of them were filled with the Holy Spirit and began to speak in other tongues as the Spirit enabled them" (Acts. 2:2–4). Peter explained this miracle by the action of the Holy Spirit sent to them by Jesus (Acts 2:33).

The emphasis on this episode is not accidental. The apostles of nascent Christendom and the author of the Acts—Luke was one of them—needed to justify preaching about Jesus not so much among the Jews as among the Gentiles. Through the scene of the "confusion of tongues," Luke let his readers know that Jesus himself had sent the promised Comforter, the Holy Spirit, to encourage his disciples to preach the new teaching among the various nations. This episode legitimized and sanctified Paul's idea of the importance of missionary work among the Gentiles. However, Luke could not have witnessed this event (he was too young and was living in Syria) and then written about it half a century later, when the few surviving eyewitnesses of that Pentecost were already so old that their memories could be very vague and contradictory. It should be noted that the idea of preaching about Christ among the Gentiles did not arise from the disciples of Jesus, but from the educated Jews of the Diaspora, such as Paul, Barnabas, Silas, and Mark, and this idea did not appear until the end of the '40s, after the first missionary trip of the apostle Paul. In the years 27–29 CE, when Pentecost was first celebrated without Jesus, such an idea could not yet be born because the disciples and followers of Jesus saw their main task as preaching about the Messiah among their own Jewish people. But in the '60s—to the '90s, when the gospels and Acts were being created, missionary work among the pagans became the main focus of the first Christians.

In this regard, the apostle Peter, who explained to others why the Holy Spirit descended on the disciples of Jesus, did not mention the confusion of tongues but emphasized a completely different phenomenon—prophecies from the lips of the followers of Christ. Referring to the prediction of the prophet Joel, Peter believed that such a phenomenon could occur only before the end of the world, when "the sun will be turned to darkness and the moon to blood before the coming of the great and glorious day of the Lord. And everyone who calls on the name of the Lord will be saved" (Acts 2:16–21). These words of Peter indicate that the expectation of the Second Coming of Christ turned the Nazarenes into the greatest apocalyptics among all the currents of Judaism. Here the apostle also put forward another idea, which was taken up and developed later by subsequent generations of Christians, namely, that all the promises of the Lord given to King David are fulfilled and embodied in his direct descendant—Christ (Acts 2:25–32). However, this idea did not originate with Peter; it was expressed by Jesus himself, who saw in the Son of Man not only the fulfillment of biblical prophecies but also the promises of the Lord to King David.

Peter's address to the Jews of Jerusalem on the day of Pentecost contains another interesting point: In the text survives the apostle's anti-Roman statement that Jesus was killed by "wicked men who put him to death by nailing him to the cross" (Acts 2:23). But the "nailing," as well as the execution of Jesus in general, were done by the Romans, so the definition of "wicked men" refers explicitly to them. The copyists of the second century, who emasculated all the anti-Roman episodes in the New Testament, probably decided not to correct these words, hoping that after a mass of anti-Jewish inserts, the reader will consider the Jews "wicked" and not the Romans.

Before the Sanhedrin

The first serious test for the Nazarene community was the trial of the Sanhedrin over its leaders—Peter and John (Zebedee). The reason for the trial was the healing of a lame person from birth. Peter relieved him of his limp "in the name of Jesus Christ of Nazareth" in the presence of John, and the crowd gathered at the entrance to the Temple in Jerusalem. The rumor of the miraculous healing of the lame man spread like lightning among the worshippers in the Temple, and a multitude of enthusiastic Jews surrounded the leaders of the Nazarenes. However, Peter immediately admitted that the lame man was healed not by his own "power or piety," but by faith in Jesus Christ. Peter then began to preach in the

Temple about Jesus and his resurrection from the dead, which caused the dissatisfaction of the priests. As a result of the conflict with them, Peter and John were "put in jail until the next day," until the Sanhedrin met and decided their fate (Acts 3:1–16; 4:1–3). The Temple priests were concerned not so much with the preaching of the resurrection of the dead, which they, like all Sadducees, never acknowledged, as with the messianic expectations of the Nazarene leaders. The messianism of the Nazarenes found a lively response among the Jewish people, and any rumor of the appearance of the Messiah threatened unrest and clashes with the Romans, for whom the Messiah was just a new "king of the Jews," hostile to the power of Rome.

Saint Peter of Rubens. 1610-1612.

It was not until the next day that the Temple priests were able to convene a meeting of the Sanhedrin (apparently, a small one of 23 people). However, the court found no fault in the actions of Peter and John and released them. The judges "could not decide how to punish them, because all the people were praising God for what had happened" (Acts 4:21). The healing of the lame man and the acquittal of the Sanhedrin strengthened the authority of the Nazarenes and their leaders, which contributed to the rapid growth of the community and its influence among the inhabitants of Jerusalem (Acts 4:4; 5:13–14). Feeling the support of the Jewish people, the leaders of the Nazarenes, and especially Peter, again challenged the Sadducee priests, resuming their preaching in the Temple. In response, a new arrest followed, and until the next trial, the leaders of the Nazarenes were put in the public jail. However, the apostles were released very quickly. The Acts attribute this quick release to the actions of an angel of the Lord who "opened the doors of the jail and brought them out" (Acts 5:18–19). In reality, however, this angel of the Lord was the same Jewish people who shared the messianic aspirations of the Nazarenes and did not allow the Sadducee priests to condemn Peter and John.

The new court was forced to take into account the fact that the leaders of the Nazarenes had the full support of the inhabitants of Jerusalem, which allowed them not only to escape from the jail, but the next day to defiantly continue preaching in the Temple against the will of the priests. The Acts indicate that the Temple guards and servants brought Peter and John for trial, but "they did not use force, because they feared that the people would stone them" (Acts 5:26). This time the court session was more than short. Despite the Sadducees' anger at the preaching of the resurrection of Jesus from the dead, the fear of popular unrest overcame their desire to deal with the rebellious Nazarenes. In addition, the Pharisees, who made up a significant part of the Sanhedrin, refused to judge the Nazarenes, who were spiritually close to them, especially with regard to their messianic expectations and the idea of resurrection from the dead. The leader of the Pharisees in the Sanhedrin, the well-known teacher of the law Gamaliel the Elder, spoke in defense of Peter and John as follows: "I advise you: Leave these men alone! Let them go! For if their purpose or activity is of human origin, it will fail. But if it is from God, you will not be able to stop these men; you will only find yourselves fighting against God" (Acts 5:38–39). Given the mood of the Jewish people, the members of the Sanhedrin had no choice but to accept Gamaliel's opinion and release the Nazarene leaders. When the disciples of Jesus began to preach again in the Jerusalem Temple the next day, the Sadducee priests no longer dared to interfere with them.

The acquittal of the Sanhedrin legitimized the position of the Nazarenes as an independent, and most importantly, bona fide religious community in Judea. From this point on, the Nazarenes—the first Christians—became another form of Judaism, along with the Pharisees, Sadducees, and Essenes. From a religious point of view, the Nazarenes certainly distinguished themselves and broke with the Pharisees, to whom they formerly belonged, but they had not yet moved beyond the broad field of Judaism. Peter and John, like all the members of their community, considered themselves to be no less true Judeans than their opponents, the Sadducees and Pharisees. They were convinced that their faith in the risen Jesus did not contradict the laws and traditions of Judaism but, indeed, only confirmed them.

Stephen—the first Christian martyr

Helping the needy and the poor has always been one of the most important Judaic laws. It became even more important among the Nazarenes, who practiced community of possessions and equality in the use of income. However, support was needed not only for the destitute people of Judea but also for the poor from the Jewish Diaspora of other countries. When distributing donations to the needy, however, there were often disagreements and complaints of injustice, so to avoid mistakes, the Nazarene community chose from among its members seven respected and knowledgeable people who were supposed to fairly divide the charitable aid between the poor of Judea and the Diaspora. In addition to the Aramaic and Hebrew languages, the chosen ones had to know Greek, the primary language of the Jewish Diaspora. Judging by the Greek names of the chosen ones, they all either lived in Hellenistic countries or constantly communicated with the Greek world. Stephen, an educated Jew from the Diaspora who had joined the Nazarene community, became responsible for the distribution of aid. Gradually, Stephen became known in Jerusalem not only as the administrator of the Nazarenes' material resources but also as a skilled orator and a stanch follower of Jesus. His extensive knowledge of the Scriptures and his eloquence earned him well-deserved recognition and, at the same time, created many personal enemies in the ranks of the Nazarenes' opponents. However, his opponents, like Stephen himself, belonged not to the local Jews of Jerusalem but to the Diaspora from the Hellenistic countries. Heated religious disputes not only glorified Stephen but also caused misfortune.

His detractors complained about him to the Sanhedrin, accusing him of "blasphemy," and Nazarene Stephen unexpectedly found himself before the supreme religious court.

According to the Acts (and this is the only source of our knowledge of Stephen), when the high priest asked him: "Are these charges true?" Stephen began his defense with a more than extensive review of Jewish history. After mentioning all the biblical patriarchs, he dwells in detail on the sojourn of the Israelites in Egypt and on the personality of Moses. But when he reaches the middle of the biblical story—before Solomon built the Temple in Jerusalem—the text of his speech suddenly breaks off and, contrary to the logic and meaning of the story, goes straight to the accusations against the court (Acts. 7:1–53). Such a sharp and incoherent transition of the text is completely atypical for the authorship of Luke, and it suggests that Stephen's speech has undergone a serious revision. It cannot be excluded that the second-century copyists, for some reason, removed the last part of his speech, leaving only the accusations against the judges. However, even from the heavily edited text that has come down to us, it can be concluded that Stephen's views on both the Jerusalem Temple and the Temple priests were much more radical than those of the apostles, the disciples of Jesus. For example, Stephen questioned the sanctity of the Temple, claiming that "the Most High does not live in houses made by men." He accused the priests: "You stiff-necked people! Your hearts and ears are still uncircumcised. You are just like your ancestors: You always resist the Holy Spirit! Was there ever a prophet your ancestors did not persecute?" (Acts 7:48,51–53). Probably, Stephen represented a more educated, and most importantly, more radical part of the Nazarene diaspora, which in its views was closer to such second-generation apostles as Paul, Silas, or Barnabas than to the disciples of Jesus. But the mere non-recognition of the authority of the Temple and the priests could not be considered blasphemy, because the Essenes also questioned the sanctity of the Temple and disrespected the Temple priests, but for this, no one accused them of blasphemy. In any case, the reader can only guess what Stephen's crime was and how he defended himself before his judges.

It is impossible not to notice that the length of Stephen's speech to the Sanhedrin exceeds that of all the others in the Acts, including the statements of Peter and Paul. Even more interesting is that from the point of view of biblical history, the text of Stephen's speech contains several errors, very strange for an educated Jew known for his victories in religious disputes. How to explain these facts? Some biblical scholars believe that Stephen's speech is a statement of the views of Luke himself, the author of the Acts, which is why it is the longest and includes errors excusable for a Gentile converted to Judaism. In addition, Luke, who wrote his Acts 40–50 years after the trial of Stephen, could not, of course, have the text of his speech before the Sanhedrin; at best, he had only heard (probably from Paul) about the views of Stephen and his tragic fate. Stephen was sentenced to death by stoning and became the first Christian martyr. However, Luke did not mention an important fact: The execution of Stephen would have been impossible without the approval of the Roman procurator. However, this anti-Roman testimony could have been removed from the text by the same copyists who "shortened" Stephen's speech. In the story of Stephen's execution, the name of the young Saul, who later became known as the apostle Paul, is mentioned for the first time. At that time, Saul endorsed the execution of the famous Nazarene and even took some part in it. This indirectly supports the assumption that Luke learned about this first Christian martyr, most likely through Paul, his older friend and mentor. Death sentences pronounced by the Sanhedrin did not need Roman approval only for a very short period of time, 41–44 CE, when power in Judea passed from the Roman procurators to the Judean king Agrippa I, the grandson of Herod the Great. But if the execution had taken place during these years, then the young Saul could not have been an opponent of Stephen since he himself had already become a Christian. Most likely, the time of the stoning of Stephen fell in the first half of the '30s CE.

The execution of Stephen led to the escape of his radical supporters among the Nazarenes from Judea but did not affect the apostles—the disciples of Jesus—and the leaders of the Jerusalem Christian community (Acts. 8:1). This fact suggests that Stephen was executed not for belonging to the followers of Christ and not for actively preaching about Jesus but for some public statements deliberately removed by the copyists from the text of the Acts.

May one baptize the Gentiles?

The first Christians in Judea felt their main task was to preach about Jesus among their own people. The Nazarenes of the Jewish Diaspora in the Hellenistic countries looked at it somewhat differently. They lived in a Gentile environment and felt it their duty to preach Christ not only to the Jews but also to those Greeks and Romans who showed an interest in Jewish monotheism. There were a lot of them then. But was it worth doing missionary work among non-Jews? While the Nazarenes in Judea were generally against the idea, the Jewish Christians in the Diaspora were clearly supportive. Jesus himself preached only among his own Jewish people. However, the gospels mention his visit to the village of Gentiles on the northeastern shore of Lake Kinneret (Sea of Galilee) in the "region of the Gerasenes." However, Jesus's attempt to start preaching there among non-Jews ended in failure. Despite the fact that he healed a mentally ill person in front of their eyes, the local Gentiles asked Christ "to leave their region" (Mark 5:1–17). From the point of view of the Gentiles, Jesus was only a Jewish prophet and had to preach among his people. And Jesus himself, as the gospels show, preferred to address only the Jews. For example, when the "Syrophoenician" woman, a Gentile from southern Lebanon, "begged Jesus to drive the demon out of her daughter," Christ gave a very interesting answer: "First let the children eat all they want; for it is not right to take the children's bread and toss it to their dogs." "Yes, Lord," she replied, "but even the dogs under the table eat the children's crumbs." Jesus appreciated these words and healed her daughter (Mark 7:25–30). This gospel episode encouraged Jews to preach about Jesus among the "God-worshippers" or "God-fearers"—those Gentiles who observed the laws of Judaism and attended synagogues. The only difference between them and the Jews was that they were born Gentiles and had not been circumcised. As we have seen, Luke, the author of the Acts and one of the gospels, came from such Gentiles. To show how it was important for non-Jews to become part of Christ, Luke emphasized that it was pleasing to the Lord himself. He dwells at length on the following vision of Peter: He "saw the heavens opened and something like a great sheet descending, being let down by its four corners upon the earth. In it were all kinds of animals and reptiles and birds of the air. And there came a voice to him: 'Rise, Peter; kill and eat.' But Peter said, 'By no means, Lord; for I have never eaten anything that is common or unclean.' And the voice came to him again a second time, 'What God has made clean, do not call common.' This happened three times, and the thing was taken up at once to heaven" (Acts 10:11–16). By this vision, the author of Acts made it clear that not only Jews can be Christians but also Gentiles, especially if they believe in the Lord. Luke puts the following words into Peter's mouth, calling for a new attitude toward Gentiles: "You yourselves know how unlawful it is for a Jew to associate with or to visit anyone of another nation, but God has shown me that I should not call any person common or unclean (Acts 10:28). In this case, it was a Roman centurion named Cornelius, who belonged to the God-worshippers and was known as "a righteous and God-fearing man, who is respected by all the Jewish people" (Acts 10:22). Peter's reaction to Cornelius's desire to be baptized and become a follower of Jesus is remarkable: "God does not show favoritism but accepts from every nation the one who fears him and does what is right. . . . Surely no one can stand in the way of their being baptized with water. They have received the Holy Spirit just as we have" (Acts 10:34–35,47). Thus, the apostle made an important decision—that non-Jewish males who wished to be baptized were not required to undergo the rite of circumcision. However, this applied only to those Gentiles who had previously accepted Jewish monotheism and observed the laws of Judaism, that is, God-fearers. Peter's position was extremely important because he was not only the leader of the Christian community but also the first important apostle chosen by Christ himself. Despite this, the baptism of uncircumcised non-Jews caused dissatisfaction among the other apostles and members of the community. "You went into the house of uncircumcised men and ate with them," they reproached him (Acts 11:3). To which Peter objected: "If God gave them the same gift he gave us who believed in the Lord Jesus Christ, who was I to think that I could stand in God's way?" However, there was no real conflict here because the joining to Christianity did not involve a pagan but rather a God-fearer who had long accepted Jewish monotheism and was "respected" by the Jews. The inclusion of such Gentiles in the Christian community did not cause serious objections, so the discontented "had no further objections and praised God, saying, so then, even to Gentiles God has granted repentance that leads to life" (Acts 11:18). The disciples of Jesus regarded the Christian community as an integral part of Jewish society and the Christian teaching as one of the currents of Judaism. From their point of view, any potential candidate for Christianity had to first convert to Judaism and fulfill all its laws and regulations, and only then could they undergo baptism. In short, without being circumcised and becoming a Jew, it was impossible to be baptized because baptism in water was considered as one of the rituals of Judaism. The case of Cornelius set a precedent in that a Gentile was allowed to be baptized without undergoing the rite of circumcision. But this happened at the insistence of the apostle Peter himself and did not change the negative attitude of the Christian community to missionary work among the Gentiles. At that time, even the radical Nazarenes, who left Judea after Stephen's execution, were not preaching about Jesus to anyone except the Jews (Acts 11:19).

Peter was not the first to start preaching among non-Jews. Probably the very first was Philip, who turned his attention to the Samaritans who lived in central Palestine. The Samaritans formed as a separate ethnic group after the destruction of Samaria (the capital of the kingdom of Israel) in 722 BCE, when the Assyrian conquerors took part of the Israelite population to Mesopotamia and in their place brought inhabitants of Mesopotamian and Syrian cities. The newcomers quickly merged with the remaining Israelites and adopted their culture and religion. Despite this, the Judeans did not recognize the Samaritans as the heirs of the northern Hebrew tribes and did not allow their pilgrims to enter the Jerusalem Temple. Thus arose a centuries-old enmity between two parts of the same people.

Peter baptizes the Roman centurion Cornelius.
A 12th-century font in St Bartholomew's Church in Liege.

At that time, the shortest route from Galilee to Jerusalem was through the land of the Samaritans. Jesus and his disciples passed through their settlements more than once but did not preach among them. The first person to tell the Samaritans about Christ was Philip. It is true that he was not one of the twelve disciples of Jesus, but his namesake, the former assistant of Stephen, the first Christian martyr, who was engaged in distributing aid to the needy. Philip was one of the radicals among the Nazarenes and escaped from Judea with them after Stephen's execution. But unlike his companions, who went to Phoenicia, Cyprus, and Antioch to preach about Jesus to the local Jews, Philip turned to the Samaritans. Acts does not mention the name of the city where he preached, but it is clear that his missionary work was so successful that Peter and John also went there. "They prayed for the new believers there that they might receive the Holy Spirit because the Holy Spirit had not yet come on any of them; they had simply been baptized in the name of the Lord Jesus" (Acts 8:15–16). Obviously, only the disciples of Christ had the right to "place their hands" on the baptized to "receive the Holy Spirit." But the baptism of the Samaritans did not present as significant a problem as the baptism of the pagans: after all, the religion of the Samaritans was only a trend of Judaism, and they, like the Jews, also practiced circumcision.

The Nazarene Philip, originally from Caesarea, turned out to be a born missionary: in addition to the Samaritans, he managed to baptize one of the highest dignitaries of the Ethiopian royal court, who had earlier joined the Jewish monotheism. According to Church tradition, his missionary work eventually took him to Asia Minor. In Christian literature, the Nazarene Philip has often been confused with another Philip, a disciple of Jesus, a fisherman from Galilee, who also, according to the Church fathers, ended his life in Asia Minor. But unlike the latter, Philip of Caesarea was well educated, fluent in Greek, and an experienced and successful missionary, and most likely it was he, and not a disciple of Jesus, who ended his days in Greek-speaking Phrygia. It was Philip of Caesarea who received the apostles Paul and Luke at his home when they returned to Jerusalem from their last missionary trip, and it was he who had four prophetic daughters (Acts 21:8–9). Perhaps Papias of Hierapolis, when he claimed to have known the daughters of Philip, was mistaken in taking him for a disciple of Jesus. It is not surprising that Papias was severely criticized by Eusebius of Caesarea for his mistakes and naivety.

The earliest experiences of missionary work by Peter and Philip among the non-Jews were with either Samaritans or what were known as "God-fearing people," those who had long lived according to the laws of Jewish monotheism. The preaching of the first Christians had not yet reached the true pagans. At this initial stage of its development, the Christian communities consisted exclusively of Jews and their missionaries preached only to Jews. From the point of view of the first Christians, in order to accept Jesus, it was necessary to abandon idolatry and to know the true God, who had been revealed only to the Jews. To come to the Lord, you had to become part of those to whom he had revealed himself—that is, to join Judaism with all its laws, traditions, and rituals. This opinion was held by all the apostles—disciples of Jesus, without exception. Only Paul, having joined the Christians, radically changed attitudes toward the Gentiles and the nature of their communion with Jesus. But the main battles over the inclusion of non-Jews in Christian communities were still to come.

A new attitude toward the Gentiles began to form in Antioch, the second Christian community after Jerusalem at that time. There, in a multi-ethnic city where Jews lived together with Greeks and Syrians, the idea of preaching about Jesus among non-Jews first arose. It is noteworthy that the name for believers in Christ—*Christians*—first appeared there; it is a Greek translation from the Hebrew, "those who believe in the Messiah." The idea of Christian missionary work among Gentiles was prompted by the fact that the Jews in general were not in a hurry to be baptized, and this was not accidental.

Why did the majority of Jewish people not accept Jesus?

How could it happen that the people who gave the world Christ did not accept him? The explanation of this paradox lies in what the biblical tradition meant by the Messiah and what it saw as his tasks. The Old Testament does not have any precise definition of the Savior, but all the prophecies of him boiled down to the belief that the Messiah, or Christ (derived from Greek), was to become the Son of Man from the lineage of David and be born in Bethlehem—the native city of the legendary king. As the messenger of God, the Messiah was to save the Jewish people from their enemies, restore the kingdom of David, and ascend his throne. And so, the Messiah was understood to be not God or his Son but a man who would be guided by the Holy Spirit in his mission. This meant defeating Israel's enemies. Upon fulfillment of his task, the Savior would become the "Judean king." Biblical tradition excluded entirely any possibility that the Messiah would not achieve victory and might suffer from his enemies. The Old Testament prophets similarly do not say anything about the "immaculate conception" of the messenger of God from the Holy Spirit; most importantly, they are totally silent regarding the humiliation, execution, and resurrection after three days of the one who was destined to become the Savior. All attempts to find hints of this in the biblical prophecies have proven unconvincing.

According to the Old Testament tradition, the Messiah had to miraculously defeat his enemies—not to perish at their hands. His resurrection three days after the execution was not predicted by any biblical prophet. Moreover, such an early physical resurrection after death did not fit at all into the understanding of even those (Pharisees), who believed in resurrection at all. The idea of being crucified for the sins of all humanity was also unknown to Judaism. Because what happened to Jesus did not correspond to the Old Testament's notions of the Messiah, in the eyes of the majority of the Jewish people, he simply did not become the Savior they were awaiting. The apostles, of course, like all the followers of Jesus, claimed that the resurrection of their Teacher served as best evidence for his being the Messiah. However, according to the same Old Testament tradition, the Messiah, whose mission was to defeat his enemies, should not have been resurrected; moreover, the resurrected Jesus "was not seen by all the people"—testified the apostle Peter—"but by witnesses whom God had already chosen," that is, only by his disciples and followers (Acts 10:41). Therefore, the main evidence for Jesus's messianic nature could not be presented to the masses of the Jewish people.

In short, Jesus was a completely different Messiah, one whose image did not correspond to the prophecies. He did not win but suffered; he did not come to restore the kingdom of David but rather to save the souls of the "perished sheep of Israel"; he did not destroy his enemies but called for them to be loved; he did not come to judge but to save; he did not bring punishment or retribution to sinners but showed them mercy and compassion. And no matter how the evangelists Matthew and Luke tried to "improve" the situation, claiming that Jesus was from the lineage of David and was born in Bethlehem, none of this changed what was important—that Jesus did not do what was demanded of him by the biblical prophecies. If even Christ's disciples were not able to understand how their Teacher could suffer from his enemies, then what was to be expected from other people? The Jewish people had hoped that they found in Jesus the long-awaited Messiah who would free them from the rule of

Roman pagans and would restore the kingdom of David. As long as the Judeans cherished these hopes, they deeply believed in Jesus and protected him. But after Christ allowed their enemies to capture, humiliate, and crucify him, the people decided that Jesus was not the Messiah that they had waited for.

After his crucifixion, Jesus's disciples and followers began to develop a new view of Christ, according to which the purpose of his coming to our world was not to end the rule of Roman pagans and restore the kingdom of David but to save the souls of his people, "the perished sheep of Israel" for the kingdom of God. This new interpretation of the Messiah's role clearly differed from that of the Old Testament and was not easily embraced by Jewish society. This circumstance obliged Jesus's followers from the educated Jewish Diaspora to move their preaching to the Gentiles. Unlike the Jews, the Gentiles did not have any problems with biblical tradition and the demands it made on the future Messiah. They were not bothered by the issue of the Messiah's nature and his role in the salvation of the Jewish people. The miracles demonstrated by Jesus and his equally incredible resurrection were sufficient to motivate the newly converted pagans to further develop the idea of Jesus's disciples, declaring him the Son of God who suffered from his enemies and died for the sins of all humanity. The image of the Son of Man, the Savior of the Jewish people who was to restore the kingdom of David, was replaced by the concept of the Son of God, the Savior of all people who suffered for the sins of our world. In this way, to the Old Testament's image of the Messiah was added a New Testament view of the Savior. The second point of view, embraced by former pagans, did not correspond at all to the first, which was adhered to by the Jews.

Already by the middle of the first century CE, there had occurred a divide in Judean society regarding Jesus. The majority of people continued to adhere to the Old Testament point of view, according to which Jesus could not be the Messiah, as he did not accomplish what was expected of the Son of Man. At the same time, a minority accepted the New Testament view on Jesus and began to preach it vigorously, wherever the Jews lived. This controversy among the Judeans took on such a heated character that the Roman emperor Claudius, despite his favorable attitude to the Jews, decided to expel all the debaters from Rome, as they created an unbearable atmosphere in the capital of the empire. The Book of Acts testifies that there were many thousands of these Jewish Christians in both Judea and the Hellenistic countries. (Acts 5:14; 6:7; 9:31; 21:20).

It was they who spread the new teaching throughout the entire ancient world and became the founders of the first Christian communities.

The fact that most Jews did not recognize Jesus as the Messiah was deemed by the apostles to be the will of God. They thought that God intentionally made it difficult for them to preach about Jesus among their brethren so that they could bring the message of salvation to all the peoples of the world.

The New Testament Book of Acts

Only one New Testament writing—The Acts of the Holy Apostles—speaks about the life of the first Christians after the crucifixion of Jesus. It is the primary, and in many ways the only, source for the history of early Christianity. The book covers a very short period of time, from the late 20s to the early 60s, no more than three and a half decades. Like all four canonical gospels, Acts is written in Koine, the colloquial Greek of the first century CE. The language and literary level of this work is very high; only the Gospel of Luke can match it. And this is not accidental, since the peculiarities of the vocabulary and style of both this gospel and the Acts point to the same author. The early Church fathers, Irenaeus of Lyons, Eusebius of Caesarea, and Tertullian, Origen, and Clement of Alexandria all speak with one voice of Luke's authorship. This is confirmed by the Latin translation of the most ancient list of New Testament writings, the so-called Muratorian Canon, which dates back to about 190 CE. Today, few biblical scholars try to challenge the widespread opinion that it is the evangelist Luke who is the author of the Acts. However, there is one circumstance that confuses researchers: The author not only omits any mention of the numerous epistles of the apostle Paul, but judging by the text, he has never read them. As Paul's assistant and companion, Luke would have known, if not of all, then at least of some of his epistles. Although it's possible, in principle, that Paul's colleague did not know about the apostle's letters, this fact does not speak in his favor. On the other hand, there is an important argument in support of Luke's authorship. In those days, authors often signed the names of those who enjoyed special respect and veneration in order to give their works greater significance. For example, the creation of two gospels is attributed to the disciples of Christ Matthew and John, although in reality, they were not their authors. However, the name of Luke, a former pagan who had known neither Jesus nor his disciples, was not surrounded by a halo of authority and universal recognition, so there was no reason to attribute to him the honor of creating a work if he did not write it. In short, Luke is the most likely author of the Acts.

It is much more difficult to determine the time of appearance of this book. Acts ends with a description of the events of the early 60s, when the apostle Paul "in bonds" arrives in Rome, where he will await trial. On this basis, some biblical scholars assign the time of creation of the work to the early 60s. However, early in his work the author (in the address to Theophilus) emphasizes that Acts are just a continuation of his first book, i.e., the Gospel of Luke, which was clearly written after 70 CE. How could the second part be created before the first? To understand this, it is necessary to pay attention to some details in the text of the Acts that suggest the author of the book was aware of the subsequent tragic events but chose not to report them. Thus, he knew not only that Paul's third missionary trip (to Greece and Asia Minor) would be his last, but also that the apostle would be executed in Rome. It is not by chance that, even before his arrest, he puts the following words into Paul's mouth: "Now I know that none of you among whom I have gone about preaching the kingdom will ever see me again" (Acts 20:25). Despite the fact that the fate of the apostle could not yet be known to anyone, and it would seem that nothing threatened him, his colleagues and friends said good-bye to him forever: "They all wept as they embraced him and kissed him. What grieved them most was his statement that they would never see his face again" (Acts 20:37–38). The author, intentionally, even before any misadventures of Paul, introduces the prophecy of Agabus into the text: " . . . a prophet named Agabus came down from Judea. Coming over to us, he took Paul's belt, tied his own hands and feet with it and said, "The Holy Spirit says, 'In this way the Jewish leaders in Jerusalem will bind the owner of this belt and will hand him over to the Gentiles'" (Acts 21:10–11).

Another thing that draws attention to itself is that the epilogue of Acts is clearly not complete. Did the author not have time to finish his work, or did the copyists perhaps remove the last part of the book because it cast a shadow on the Romans? Probably neither the first nor the second. The author himself most likely refused to complete the work because he would have had to blame Rome not only for the murder of the apostles Peter and Paul but also for the terrible tortures of the early Christians, whom the emperor Nero set wild beasts upon and threw into the fire for the amusement of the Roman crowd. From the text of the

Acts, it is easy to see that the author carefully avoided any anti-Roman statements and even hints. On the contrary, he tried in all situations to portray the Romans more than positively. His main goal was to show that nascent Christianity did not pose any threat to Roman power, and this, of course, could not be done by telling the story of the further fate of the apostles in Rome. Thus, although the Book of Acts ends its narrative with the beginning of the '60s, in reality, it was written no earlier than the '70s-'80s CE.

The title Book of Acts claims to describe the acts of many of the apostles of Christianity, but in fact, it tells only about two of them—Peter and Paul. And the focus is primarily on Paul. John Zebedee is mentioned only as a companion of Peter and then only in passing. His elder brother James is reported to have been executed on the orders of Herod Agrippa I, and with no reason given for such a harsh sentence. Concerning the other disciples of Jesus, the book is completely silent; they are listed only by name, but not a word is said about them. True, the apostles Barnabas, Silas, and Mark (from the Jewish Diaspora) are mentioned, but only in connection with Paul's missionary work. Surprisingly, much is said about Philip, Stephen's assistant in distributing aid to those in need. But Philip (who was not a disciple of Jesus) held a secondary position in the Christian community of Judea. How to explain such a strange approach by the author to covering the activity of the apostles? Why does he say nothing about the fate of the disciples of Jesus (except Peter) yet tell a very detailed story about Paul? These oddities are explained by the fact that the author of Acts, contrary to Church traditions, did not know any of the disciples of Jesus. Of the apostles of Christianity, he was well acquainted only with Paul. He may have met Barnabas and Silas in Antioch, but he was not close to them. He drew all his information about Jesus and his disciples from those Aramaic and Hebrew manuscripts that became the basis for writing the Synoptic Gospels. By the way, the apostle Paul also received his knowledge about Jesus from these records. Luke learned about the life of the Christian community in Judea after the crucifixion of Jesus and about the missionary activities of the Jewish Diaspora mainly from Paul, his friend and mentor. But Paul himself, of all the disciples of Jesus, knew only Peter and John, and even then only superficially. He knew Barnabas much better; Barnabas had been a great help to him during his conversion to Christianity and had been his faithful companion during his first missionary journey through Cyprus and Asia Minor. Thus, apart from scant information about Peter and John, Luke had no information about the other disciples of Jesus. He knew a great deal about Paul, from the apostle's own mouth. This is why his Book of Acts is devoted mainly to Paul, speaks far less about Peter, very sparingly mentions James and John, and is completely silent about the rest of the apostles. It is true that Luke tells a little about Barnabas and Silas, but only what he heard about them from Paul. Special attention is given to Philip because the author, together with Paul, visited his home in Caesarea, so he had the opportunity to get to know him personally and learn about both his preaching in Samaria and the baptism of a dignitary of the Ethiopian court. Most likely, it was from Philip that the author received new details about the trial of Stephen, in addition to what Paul had told him. Thanks to Luke, we have at least some information about the brother of Jesus—James, who, along with Peter, was one of the leaders of the Christian community in Judea. However, this information also came to Luke from Paul, since the author of the Acts did not know James personally.

In general, this New Testament work consists of two very unequal parts. The main and most significant part consists of the Acts of Paul and the story of his humble contacts with other followers of Jesus. In all that concerns this apostle, Luke gives truthful and quite detailed information, and this despite the fact that he clearly did not read Paul's epistles. The influence of the apostle on the author is so great that the whole book is written from the ideological position of Paul. Much more problematic is the case with the other part of the book, which deals with the Christian community of Judea and the disciples of Jesus. Here Luke tells us very little and only what he has learned from others, usually from the same Paul. But Paul, by his own admission, was "unknown to the churches of Judea," and he himself had little idea of their real life. This could not but affect the book of Luke, so in everything that concerns the Christians of Judea and the disciples of Jesus, the text is fragmentary, has extensive gaps and sometimes contains inaccurate information. We must not forget that the Acts, like the gospels, are not a documentary historical chronicle but a literary work (although based on real facts), so the book cannot claim to adequately reflect events.

PART FOUR

The apostle Paul—the founder of Christianity

"I have begotten you in Christ Jesus by the gospel." (1 Cor. 4:15)

IN TERMS OF HIS importance in the history of Christianity, the apostle Paul ranks second after Jesus Christ. It was Paul who created a new religion based on the fact of the resurrection of Christ, and his views decided the shape of this religion. Only he decided what should be borrowed from Judaism and what should not. The development of Christianity actually pushed aside all the disciples and companions of Jesus, including such apostles as Peter, James, and John because their faith in Jesus did not go beyond the framework of traditional Judaism. And although the birth of Christianity is sanctified by the authority of the biblical prophets and all the apostles of Jesus, the true and only father of the new religion was, in reality, Paul. Who was this brilliant visionary who defined the religious views of European civilization?

The zealous Pharisee

Paul was born around 10 CE in the ancient Cilician city of Tarsus, located in southeastern Asia Minor (today's Turkey). It was a Hellenistic city, then belonging to the Roman Empire. About his origin, Paul himself writes as follows: "circumcised on the eighth day, of the people of Israel, of the tribe of Benjamin, a Hebrew of Hebrews; in regard to the law, a Pharisee" (Phil. 3:5). His original Jewish name was Saul (Shaul), only later he added to it a second, Latin name—Paul ("small"). Saul's family was not rich and earned their living by their own labor, making and selling tents made of leather. Despite this, Saul's father managed to obtain Roman citizenship for the whole family, which was then very valuable and expensive. Apparently, even in Tarsus, the boy received a dual education: Hellenistic and Jewish. But Saul's father wanted more. He finds money to send his son to study in Judea with the famous Pharisee and Torah scholar Gamaliel the Elder. We do not know how long Saul studied in Jerusalem, but judging by his extensive knowledge of the Scriptures, he received good training.

In those years, a new trend in Judaism emerged from the Pharisees—the Nazarenes. Their main difference from the Pharisees was their belief in Jesus as the Jewish Messiah, who came to save the people of Israel but was crucified by the Romans. The Nazarenes claimed that Jesus rose again on the third day and appeared repeatedly among his disciples for forty days. This group held apocalyptic views—that is, they believed in the imminent end of our world, the return of the Messiah, and his judgment on all humanity. In theological terms, the Nazarenes differed from the Pharisees in only two aspects: First, they understood the nature and role of the Messiah differently, and second, they interpreted the laws of the Oral Torah more liberally, following the example of their Teacher. Judaism of that time, however, like today, was not a monolithic doctrine, and the appearance of another trend in it did not change much in the religious atmosphere of Judea. However, the young educated Pharisees (guided by today's terminology, they could be called "fundamentalists") reacted to the split of their religious school very painfully, and to the Nazarenes hostilely. Among such young and ideologically irreconcilable Pharisees, Saul occupied a prominent place. Much later, in his epistle "To the Galatians", Paul confessed: "For you have heard of my previous way of life in Judaism, how intensely I persecuted the church of God and tried to destroy it. I was advancing in Judaism beyond many of my own age among my people and was extremely zealous for the traditions of my fathers" (Gal. 1:13–14). The Acts, in recounting that Saul was on the side of those who judged and then executed the first Christian martyr, Stephen (Acts 7:58; 8:1), reminds us what a zealous Pharisee he was.

However, just as Paul himself was overly critical of the mistakes of his youth, so the Acts clearly overreacted in portraying the cruelties of his Pharisaic past. Therefore, the following quotation from the same Acts should be considered as an exaggeration of what the apostle did in relation to the Nazarenes: "But Saul began to destroy the church. Going from house to house, he dragged off both men and women and put them in prison" (Acts 8:3). We must not forget that Judaism of that time represented different religious schools, which at the same time quite peacefully coexisted with each other. Obviously, the atmosphere of violence depicted here is clearly taken from another time and place.

Communion with Jesus

A sharp turn in the life and outlook of Paul occurred completely unexpectedly and inexplicably. This happened on the way from Jerusalem to Damascus, where Saul intended to continue his struggle with the Nazarenes. The Acts narrate this in the following way: "As he neared Damascus on his journey, suddenly a light from heaven flashed around him. He fell to the ground and heard a voice say to him, 'Saul, Saul, why do you persecute me?' 'Who are you, Lord?' Saul asked. 'I am Jesus, whom you are persecuting,' he replied. 'Now get up and go into the city, and you will be told what you must do.' The men traveling with Saul stood there speechless; they heard the sound but did not see anyone. Saul got up from the ground, but when he opened his eyes he could see nothing. So they led him by the hand into Damascus. For three days he was blind, and did not eat or drink anything" (Acts 9:3–9). In Damascus, the blind Saul was helped to regain his sight by the Jew Ananias, who was a believer in Jesus. From this point on, Saul joined Jesus and became one of the Nazarenes whom he used to persecute mercilessly.

According to the Acts, Saul returned from Damascus to Jerusalem, where he tried in vain to become a member of the Nazarene community; however, they do not trust him, remembering his former views. It is difficult to say what would have been the fate of Saul if not for the help of Barnabas, a Jew from Cyprus who was trusted by the disciples of Jesus. Barnabas brought Saul to the apostles Peter, James, and John and vouched for him, confirming what had happened to him on the way to Damascus. But Saul did not stay long in Jerusalem. For some unknown reason, his fellow countrymen, pilgrims from Asia Minor (Hellenists), began to conflict with him, and in order to avoid the worst, the Jerusalem Nazarene community sent Saul to his native Tarsus. After a while, the same Barnabas came for him and invited him to his home in Antioch (northern Syria). So Saul became a permanent member of the Antioch community, which was the first to call itself "Christian" (Acts. 9:26–30;

11:25). From this time on, Saul became known to everyone by his second, Latin name as Paul.

From this more than scanty information in Acts, we are unable to determine where and from whom Paul received his knowledge of Jesus and his teaching. After all, Paul appeared in Jerusalem after the crucifixion of Jesus, so he had never seen or heard the Messiah. Moreover, he knew almost none of Jesus's disciples, and this at a time when none of the canonical gospels known to us had yet been written! Fortunately, we have another important source of information about Paul—his personal epistles, where he writes about his communion with Christ. In the epistle to the Galatians, the apostle makes the stunning admission that after believing in Jesus, he did not go to the apostles in Jerusalem to gain more knowledge of Jesus and his teaching. It was only three years later that he went to Jerusalem to meet the apostle Peter, and even then, he stayed with him for only 15 days. He saw no one but the apostles Peter and James (the brother of Jesus)! (Gal. 1:17–21). Paul does not hide the fact that he did not learn from any of the first Christians: "I was personally unknown to the churches of Judea that are in Christ. They only heard the report: "The man who formerly persecuted us is now preaching the faith he once tried to destroy" (Gal.1:22–23). Thus, Paul's personal memoirs do not fully confirm the information from the Acts.

Then how did Paul learn about the teaching of Jesus? The apostle claims that he received the teaching of Jesus from Christ himself, through his revelation to him. Moreover, after receiving a revelation from Jesus himself, Paul, according to his own account, did not consult with any of the people and did not go to the apostles, the disciples of Jesus. "But when God, who set me apart from my mother's womb and called me by his grace, was pleased to reveal his Son in me so that I might preach him among the Gentiles, my immediate response was not to consult any human being. I did not go up to Jerusalem to see those who were apostles before I was, but I went into Arabia. Later I returned to Damascus" (Gal.1:15–17). Paul called himself an apostle, "sent not from men nor by a man, but by Jesus Christ and God the Father, who raised him from the dead." Therefore, Paul emphasized: "The gospel I preached is not of human origin. I did not receive it from any man, nor was I taught it; rather, I received it by revelation from Jesus Christ" (Gal. 1: 1,11–12).

However, the "revelations" that Paul received from Jesus himself could not give him comprehensive information about the life and teachings of the Son of Man. As a rule, such visions and revelations are short-lived and help a person only to make the right choice. What is the real source of Paul's knowledge of Jesus? As one of the most diligent students of Gamaliel the Elder, Paul could not help but get acquainted with those manuscripts in Aramaic and Hebrew that were later used to write the canonical gospels in Greek. No serious biblical scholar doubts that such manuscripts actually existed. Even as a zealous Pharisee, Paul could not help but be interested in the "Christian heresy" of his ideological opponents. It was these manuscripts about the life of the Messiah and his resurrection that most likely changed Paul's worldview. The revelation of Christ on the road to Damascus completed the revolution in his views and made him an ascetic in the cause of Jesus.

Preaching among Jews and Gentiles

The idea of preaching the gospel of Christ among Gentiles did not arise easily or immediately. This was because Jesus himself considered the main task of his earthly life to be "the salvation of the lost sheep of Israel" and directed his sermons exclusively to the Jewish people. Naturally, his disciples and followers, mindful of the instructions of the Messiah, tried to continue his work only among their own people. The idea of bringing Gentiles to Christ applied at first to what were known as God-fearing people, not to pagans in general. This category of non-Jews, disillusioned with pagan gods and idolatry, worshiped the God of Israel, attended synagogues, and tried to lead a Jewish lifestyle. The Acts report that the apostle Peter had already introduced such God-worshippers as the Roman centurion Cornelius and his soldiers. But preaching the gospel of Christ among "those who honor and fear God" was not much different from preaching among the Jews, for the former had in effect already become Jews.

For the first time, it was not the Jews of Judea who began to preach about Christ among the Gentiles, but the Jews of the Diaspora, who themselves lived among the Gentiles and knew their languages. The Book of Acts indicates that it was the Jews of Cyprus and Cyrenaica who were the first to preach about Jesus among the Hellenes, particularly in Antioch (Acts 11:20). It was in Antioch that the most famous preachers among the Gentiles gathered: Barnabas, Paul, and Silas. It is no coincidence that the first mixed Christian community (of Jews and Gentiles) appeared in this city. Of course, the Gentiles were no less a problem for Christian preachers than the Jews were. But preaching among the pagans could potentially bring incomparably greater results than preaching among the Jews in the Diaspora. After all, pagans made up the vast majority of the population, and the real power was in their hands. But how to attract the Gentiles to Christ, and most importantly, what to demand from them and what not? The preachers did not know. After all, the first Christian communities consisted almost exclusively of Jews. At that time, the prevailing opinion was that anyone who wanted to join Christ must first become a Jew, that is, convert to Judaism. But the Gentiles were deterred by the complexity of Judaic laws. The God-worshippers or God-fearing best illustrate this problem. These people, usually from the most educated part of local population, had already accepted the one God of Israel, but the requirement of circumcision kept many of them from formally converting to Judaism. In an attempt to solve this problem, Paul began to assert at his own risk that faith in Jesus exempted Gentiles from the need to fulfill the laws of Moses. At first, he freed the Gentiles from the burden of Judaic laws, but wanting to be consistent and create a single Christian community, he went much further—he began to free the Jews from their historical heritage. The idea that one could become a Christian without first becoming a Jew seemed wild and seditious at the time; thus many of the first Christians opposed Paul's sermons. In his epistle to the Galatians, the apostle drew attention to the fact that he was being persecuted precisely because he freed Gentile converts from the difficult Judaic laws, most importantly from the need for circumcision, and that this was the advantage of his preaching. If new converts were also required to be circumcised, then "the offense of the cross [that is, its salvific power] has been abolished" (Gal.5:11).

Paul made three missionary trips—to Cyprus, Asia Minor, and Greece—where he preached about Jesus to three different groups of his listeners: Jews, God-fearing Gentiles, and pagans. To understand the essence and nature of the apostle's gospel, it is worth paying attention to one of his very first sermons in Antioch of Pisidia during his first missionary trip. Paul himself found it necessary to highlight the following:

1) Jesus is a direct descendant of King David;
2) His coming was foretold by John the Baptist: "He is coming after me, whose sandals I am not worthy to untie";
3) The crucifixion of Jesus was the fulfillment of the biblical prophecies—that is, the execution of Jesus does not discredit him as the Messiah of the Jewish people;

4) God raised Jesus from the dead;

5) Jesus appeared for many days to his disciples, "who are now his witnesses before the people";

6) King David was the most faithful servant of the Lord, but "he fell asleep; he was buried with his fathers and his body decayed. But the one whom God raised from the dead did not see decay." He is the true Messiah;

7) Faith in Jesus saves a person. "Through Jesus the forgiveness of sins is proclaimed to you. Through him everyone who believes is set free from every sin, a justification you were not able to obtain under the law of Moses" (Acts 13:23–39).

One of the first images of apostle Paul. Wall
mural from Ephesus. 5th century.

This sermon is intended for only two categories of listeners—Jews and God-worshippers, since it requires at least a minimal knowledge of the Scriptures, which the pagans did not possess. Most likely, it was the God-worshippers among Gentiles who became Paul's main audience and his future flock. But the most important point is that Paul exempts not only the God-worshippers among Gentiles but also the Jews themselves from following the laws of Judaism. The condition of this liberation is absolute faith in Jesus. In turn, faith in Jesus as the true Messiah is based solely on the fact of his resurrection. Here is the prologue to a new religion built on the foundation of Judaism.

Paul considered the meaning of his life "to be a minister of Christ Jesus to the Gentiles" (Rom.15:16). This vocation he regarded as a grace given to him by God. "Although I am less than the least of all God's people, this grace was given me: to preach to the Gentiles the unsearchable riches of Christ" (Eph.3:8). In the eyes of Paul, the preaching among the Gentiles had a special significance because it was about the salvation of their souls. "For you were once darkness," Paul explained to the former Gentiles. "Remember that at that time you were separate from Christ, excluded from citizenship in Israel and foreigners to the covenants of the promise, without hope and without God in the world" (Eph. 5:8; 2:12). At the same time, Paul did not forget to preach among the Jews themselves. The fact that Paul, who rejected circumcision for the Gentiles, circumcised his assistant, the half-Jewish Timothy, during his second missionary trip, suggests that the apostle never gave up preaching among the Jews of the Diaspora. After all, an uncircumcised Timothy with a non-Jewish father would not be trustworthy enough to preach among the Jews.

Paul was very ambivalent about his role as an apostle of Jesus. On the one hand, he belittled himself by saying: "For I am the least of the apostles and do not even deserve to be called an apostle, because I persecuted the church of God." On the other hand, he acknowledged: "But by the grace of God I am what I am, and his grace to me was not without effect. No, I worked harder than all of them." However, as a modest man, he added a qualification: "Yet not I, but the grace of God that was with me" (1 Cor.15:9–10). Speaking about his apostolate, Paul emphasized that he preached the gospel of Christ free of charge. "The Lord has commanded that those who preach the gospel should receive their living from the gospel. But I have not used any of these rights" (1 Cor. 9:14–15).

In choosing the routes for his missionary journeys, Paul was guided by the following principle: "It has always been my ambition to preach the gospel where Christ was not known, so that I would not be building on someone else's foundation. Rather, as it is written: 'Those who were not told about him will see, and those who have not heard will understand'" (Rom. 15:20–21).

The results of Paul's missionary work were more than impressive: "I will not venture to speak of anything except what Christ has accomplished through me in leading the Gentiles to obey God by what I have said and done— by the power of signs and wonders, through the power of the Spirit of God. So from Jerusalem all the way around to Illyricum, I have fully proclaimed the gospel of Christ" (Rom. 15:18–19). "I have become all things to all men so that by all possible means I might save some" (1 Cor. 9:22).

Speaking about the nature of his sermon, Paul noted: "My message and my preaching were not with wise and persuasive words, but with a demonstration of the Spirit's power, so that your faith might not rest on human wisdom, but on God's power. . . . For the wisdom of this world is foolishness in God's sight . . . The Lord knows that the thoughts of the wise are futile" (1 Cor. 2:4–5; 3:19–20). Paul, as an orator, was not very strong; he could not be called eloquent. This is also supported by the apostle's own confessions. For example, in the second epistle to the Corinthians, Paul quotes a critic who, referring to the apostle, claims that "his letters are weighty and forceful, but in person he is unimpressive and his speaking amounts to nothing" (2 Cor. 10:10). Paul's failure in Athens was probably due to his lack of eloquence. Faced there with skilled pagan orators, he failed to win over the fathers of that city and was forced to leave Athens with nothing.

Paul admitted that the fate of the apostle of Christ was incredibly difficult and dangerous. "For it seems to me that God has put us apostles on display at the end of the procession, like those condemned to die in the arena. We have been made a spectacle to the whole universe, to angels as well as to human beings. We are fools for Christ, but you are so wise in Christ! We are weak, but you are strong! You are honored, we are dishonored! To this very hour we go hungry and thirsty, we are in rags, we are brutally treated, we are homeless. We work hard with our own hands. When we are cursed, we bless; when we are persecuted, we endure it; when we are slandered, we answer kindly. We have become the scum of the earth, the garbage of the world—right up to this moment" (1 Cor. 4:9–13). "For I have learned to be content whatever the circumstances. I know what it is to be in need, and I know what it is to have plenty. I have learned the secret of being content in any and every situation, whether well fed or hungry, whether living in plenty or in want" (Philip. 4:11–12). In addition to the physical and moral suffering caused to him by other people, Paul was also suffering from some kind of illness, which greatly hindered him.

> I was given a thorn in my flesh, a messenger of Satan, to torment me. Three times I pleaded with the Lord to take it away from me. But

he said to me, "My grace is sufficient for you, for my power is made perfect in weakness." Therefore I will boast all the more gladly about my weaknesses, so that Christ's power may rest on me. That is why, for Christ's sake, I delight in weaknesses, in insults, in hardships, in persecutions, in difficulties. For when I am weak, then I am strong. (2 Cor. 12: 7–10)

The arbitrary revision of the Acts by the second-century copyists changed the names of those who obstructed Paul's preaching in his three missionary journeys in Asia Minor and Greece. All Judean opponents of the apostle were called "Jews" by copyists. But the Gentile enemies of Paul are referred to not by their ethnic origin but by their first names or by the city they're from—for example, the "Ephesians" who were led by the "silversmith Demetrius" against Paul and his sermons. This is despite the fact that only the Jews gave Paul the right to preach about Jesus in their synagogues. Such a sermon in Greek temples might have cost the apostle his life. And it was the Jews, not the newly converted Gentiles, who were Paul's chief helpers in his missionary journeys. The apostle was beaten almost to death, for example, in Lystra, not by Jews but by pagan Hellenes. And in the city of Philippi (eastern Macedon), the apostles Paul and Silas were put in prison again not by the Jews but by the Macedonians. And in Athens, Paul was mocked as a "babbler" not by the Jews but by the same Gentiles (Acts 17:18). Those among the Jews who were really dissatisfied with Paul's calls to renounce all national and religious heritage tried only to refute him, while the pagan Hellenes were ready to kill the apostle for much less, as Demetrius's rebellion at Ephesus showed.

Paul's worldview

Paul believed that a human being is a hopelessly sinful creature, and in support of this point of view, referred to Scripture:

There is no one righteous, not even one; there is no one who understands; there is no one who seeks God. All have turned away, they have together become worthless; there is no one who does good, not even one. Their throats are open graves; their tongues practice deceit. The poison of vipers is on their lips. Their mouths are full of cursing and bitterness. Their feet are swift to shed blood; ruin and misery mark their ways, and the way of peace they do not know. There is no fear of God before their eyes.

In a word, the apostle concludes, "for all have sinned and fall short of the glory of God" (Rom. 3:10–18,23). But even those who try to keep the Mosaic laws will not be able to fulfill it completely. The laws of Judaism are so complex and numerous that a person of flesh and blood is simply not able to fulfill them properly. If this is the case, then all people are more or less sinful before the law, so "that a man is not justified by observing the law" (Gal. 2:16). Where is the exit? From Paul's point of view, this solution was first found with the coming of Jesus Christ, whose resurrection proved that he was the true Messiah, the Son of God, whose coming was predicted by the biblical prophets. Only sincere faith in Jesus can save a person's soul and not scrupulous observance of the numerous laws of Judaism. Paul writes:

> We who are Jews by birth and not sinful Gentiles know that a person is not justified by the works of the law, but by faith in Jesus Christ. So we, too, have put our faith in Christ Jesus that we may be justified by faith in Christ and not by the works of the law, because by the works of the law no one will be justified. (Gal. 2:15–16).

The apostle emphasizes that "it was not through the law that Abraham and his offspring received the promise that he would be heir of the world, but through the righteousness that comes by faith" (Rom. 4:13). In a word, after the resurrection of Jesus, it makes no sense to observe the laws and regulations of Judaism because faith in Jesus itself exempts from the requirements of the laws of Moses. This point of view was in sharp contrast to the position of all the disciples of Jesus, who believed Jesus's resurrection and faith in him did not exempt Jews from observing the laws of Moses. In a completely different category were converted Gentiles, who could be exempted from observing the Judaic laws but even then not from all of them. It is noteworthy that Jesus himself during his earthly life as well as after the resurrection did not exempt his disciples, as well as his people, from observing the laws of Moses. Yes, Jesus was very liberal about obedience to the instructions of the Oral Torah, believing that they came from people, not from God, but he always strictly demanded compliance with the laws of the Written Torah, that is, the legislation of Moses. Paul was certainly right when he claimed that it was impossible to be righteous according to the law. It is not without reason that a psalm of David asks: "Who can discern his errors?" (Psalm 19:12). But if righteousness cannot be achieved by strict compliance with the law, does this mean that the law should be abolished altogether? And is it possible to not comply with the laws of Judaism, which were supported and even strengthened by Christ himself? The very first psalm of the Book of Psalms emphasizes the importance of the religious law for human beings: "Blessed is the one who does not walk in step with the wicked or stand in the way that sinners take or sit in the company of mockers, but whose delight is in the law of the Lord, and who meditates on his law day and night" (Psalm 1:1). Unlike Paul, the disciples of Jesus believed that the observance of the laws of Judaism by Jews could not contradict even the deepest faith in Christ.

Thus, faith in Jesus, according to Paul, was to replace the Judaic laws, whose power was forced and temporary: "Before the coming of this faith, we were held in custody under the law, locked up until the faith that was to come would be revealed. So the law was our guardian until Christ came that we might be justified by faith. Now that this faith has come, we are no longer under a guardian" (Gal. 3: 23). When Paul extended this statement to the Gentiles, he met with no serious opposition from the other apostles—disciples of Christ. But any attempt to attribute the same to the Jews caused complete misunderstanding among the companions of Jesus. Paul's idea was tempting to Gentiles who wanted to become Christians, but it was unacceptable to most Jews. In fact, Paul, on the one hand, and the disciples of Jesus—the apostles Peter, John, and James—on the other, offered completely different interpretations of Christianity. The disciples of Jesus remained faithful to traditional Judaism and tried only to enrich it with the teaching about the life, crucifixion, and resurrection of the Jewish Messiah (Christ). In contrast, Paul preached an actual rejection of Judaism, not only for the Gentiles but also for the Jews themselves. He proposed a new religion based on the fact of the resurrection of Jesus. He replaced the teaching of Christ, which was one of the trends of Judaism, with the teaching about Christ that completely abolished the laws of Moses. From all of Judaism, Paul selected for Christians only the God of Israel, Jewish morality based on the Sinai commandments, and the books of the Old Testament (Tanakh).

It did not matter to Paul whether Jesus was born in Bethlehem or Nazareth or whether he was born of the Holy Spirit or of an ordinary man. The main thing for him was that Jesus had the Holy Spirit in him and was "the image of God" (2 Cor. 4:4). Moreover, Paul made the central point of his sermon not so much the teaching of Christ as the fact of his resurrection. Paul wrote in the first epistle to the Corinthians: "If Christ has not been raised, our preaching is useless and so is your faith. More than that, we are then found to be false witnesses about God, for we have testified about God that he raised Christ from the dead" (1 Cor. 15:14–15). In another epistle to the Romans, Paul emphasized: "And if the Spirit of him who raised Jesus from the dead is living in you, he who raised Christ from the dead will also give life to your mortal bodies because of his Spirit who lives in you" (Rom. 8:11).

About two worlds and the fate of man

Paul believed that the spirit of man finds pleasure in the laws of God. "For in my inner being I delight in God's law; but I see another law at work in me, waging war against the law of my mind and making me a prisoner of the law of sin at work within me. . . . So then, I myself in my mind am a slave to God's law, but in my sinful nature a slave to the law of sin" (Rom 7:22–23,25). According to Paul, the human body obeys the laws of the material world, where, even if limited, the "prince" of this earthly world rules, but the spirit strives to live according to the laws of another, God's world, which creates an irreconcilable contradiction within each of us. Paul lamented: "What a wretched man I am! Who will rescue me from this body that is subject to death?" (Rom. 7:24).

Paul drew attention to the fact that in our material world, when we are placed in a physical body, we are actually removed from the Lord:

> Therefore we are always confident and know that as long as we are at home in the body we are away from the Lord . . . We are confident, I say, and would prefer to be away from the body and at home with the Lord. So we make it our goal to please him, whether we are at home in the body or away from it. For we must all appear before the judgment seat of Christ, so that each of us may receive what is due us for the things done while in the body, whether good or bad. (2 Cor. 5:6,8–10)

Paul wrote in the second epistle to the Corinthians:

> For we know that if the earthly tent we live in is destroyed, we have a building from God, an eternal house in heaven, not built by

human hands. Meanwhile we groan, longing to be clothed instead with our heavenly dwelling, because when we are clothed, we will not be found naked. For while we are in this tent, we groan and are burdened, because we do not wish to be unclothed but to be clothed instead with our heavenly dwelling, so that what is mortal may be swallowed up by life. Now the one who has fashioned us for this very purpose is God, who has given us the Spirit as a deposit, guaranteeing what is to come (2 Cor. 5:1–5).

The apostle was convinced that in our earthly world, people are doomed to suffering and pain, and only the transition to another, spiritual world, to God, can save us from torment and reward for the hardships endured. "We know that the whole creation has been groaning as in the pains of childbirth right up to the present time. Not only so, but we ourselves, who have the first fruits of the Spirit, groan inwardly as we wait eagerly for our adoption to sonship, the redemption of our bodies" (Rom. 8:22–23). In Paul's view, "our present sufferings are not worth comparing with the glory that will be revealed in us" (Rom. 8:18). However, the transition to the spiritual world is possible only for those who do not yield to the temptations of the flesh and live according to the spirit:

So I say, walk by the Spirit, and you will not gratify the desires of the flesh. For the flesh desires what is contrary to the Spirit, and the Spirit what is contrary to the flesh. They are in conflict with each other, so that you are not to do whatever you want. But if you are led by the Spirit, you are not under the law.

The acts of the flesh are obvious: sexual immorality, impurity and debauchery; idolatry and witchcraft; hatred, discord, jealousy, fits of rage, selfish ambition, dissensions, factions and envy; drunkenness, orgies, and the like (Gal. 5:16–20).

Paul repeatedly warned that those "who live like this will not inherit the kingdom of God . . . A man reaps what he sows. Whoever sows to please their flesh, from the flesh will reap destruction; whoever sows to please the Spirit, from the Spirit will reap eternal life . . . Those who belong to Christ Jesus have crucified the flesh with its passions and desires" (Gal. 5:21,24; 6:7–8). Human beings, according to the apostle, should not be a slave to their own flesh: "We have an obligation—but it is not to the flesh, to live according to it. For if you live according to the flesh, you will die; but if by the Spirit you put to death the misdeeds of the body, you will live. For those who are led by the Spirit of God are the children of God" (Rom 8:12–14). In the first epistle to the Corinthians, Paul reminds us that each of the worlds, the material and immaterial, has its own spirit. "But we have not received the spirit of this world, but the Spirit from God, that we might know what is given us from God" (1 Cor. 2:12).

Mosaic portrait of apostle Paul. Archiepiscopal
Chapel in Ravenna, Italy. 494-519.

Paul warned his flock that the material world is full of evil and injustice. "Everyone who wants to live a godly life in Christ Jesus will be persecuted, while evildoers and impostors will go from bad to worse, deceiving and being deceived" (2 Tim. 3:12–13). The apostle believed that evil has so flooded the earthly world that it is impossible to avoid any contact with it. In this regard, his words from the first epistle to the Corinthians are very remarkable: "I wrote to you in my letter not to associate with sexually immoral people— not at all meaning the people of this world who are immoral, or the greedy and swindlers, or idolaters. In that case you would have to leave this world" (1 Cor. 5:9–10).

About the imminent end of the material world

Like the disciples of Jesus, as well as all the first Christians, Paul was an apocalyptic: He believed in the imminent end of our earthly world. Speaking about its perishable and transient nature, he reminded: "The time is short. From now on those who have wives should live as if they do not; those who mourn, as if they did not; those who are happy, as if they were not; those who buy something, as if it were not theirs to keep; those who use the things of the world, as if not engrossed in them. For this world in its present form is passing away" (1 Cor. 7:29–31). There are two versions of the signs of the approaching end of the world in the Pauline epistles. According to one of them, set forth in the first letter to the Thessalonians, the apostle writes the following: "About times and dates we do not need to write to you, for you know very well that the day of the Lord will come like a thief in the night. While people are saying, 'Peace and safety,' destruction will come on them suddenly, as labor pains on a pregnant woman, and they will not escape" (1 Thess. 5:1–3). This version fully corresponds to what Jesus said about the imminent end of our earthly world. Another version can be found in the second epistle to Timothy, Paul's assistant and associate. Here the apostle warns that "there will be terrible times in the last days. People will be lovers of themselves, lovers of money, boastful, proud, abusive, disobedient to their parents, ungrateful, unholy, without love, unforgiving, slanderous, without self-control, brutal, not lovers of the good, treacherous, rash, conceited, lovers of pleasure rather than lovers of God— having a form of godliness but denying its power" (2 Tim. 3:1–5). The same idea is further developed in Paul's second epistle to the Thessalonians, in which the apostle warns the Church not to give in to false rumors about the end of the world and the Second Coming of Christ. "Concerning the coming of our Lord Jesus Christ and our being gathered to him, we ask you, brothers and sisters, not to become easily unsettled or alarmed by the teaching allegedly from us—whether by a prophecy or by word of mouth or by letter—asserting that the day of the Lord has already come" (2 Thess. 2:2). In this letter, Paul expresses the idea that before the end of the world and the coming of Jesus, some global social cataclysm must occur, which will lead to the power of the evil force, and the son of the devil, posing as a messenger of God, will stand at the head of everything, including the Temple. "Don't let anyone deceive you in any way, for that day will not come until the rebellion occurs and the man of lawlessness is revealed, the man doomed to destruction. He will oppose and will exalt himself over everything that is called God or is worshiped, so that he sets himself up in God's temple, proclaiming himself to be God" (2 Thess. 2:3–4). Paul warns that the coming of Satan's messenger will be accompanied by "all kinds of counterfeit miracles, signs and wonders" and the deceived people will believe the lie. "And then the lawless one will be revealed, whom the Lord Jesus will overthrow with the breath of his mouth and destroy by the splendor of his coming" (2 Thess. 2:8). According to Paul, "the secret power of lawlessness is already at work, but the one who now holds it back will continue to do so till he is taken out of the way" (2 Thess. 2:5,7). The apostle does not reveal this in his epistle, but refers to the fact that he spoke about it when he preached in Thessalonica: "Don't you remember that when I was with you I used to tell you these things? And now you know what is holding him back, so that he may be revealed at the proper time" (2 Thess.2:5–6). This second version of Paul about the signs of the end of our world is in tune with what John the Evangelist writes in his Revelation and what many Christians believed in at the end of the first and second centuries CE. And this is not accidental, because according to most biblical scholars, both epistles 2 Timothy and 2 Thessalonians were written not by Paul himself but by his associates after the apostle's death. Therefore, if we want to know Paul's true view about the end of the world, we should accept the first version, which is set out in 1 Thessalonians, where no one doubts Paul's authorship.

Thus, Paul, being sure of the imminent end of the world, did not know its time or its signs, but neither did the disciples of Jesus. However, what to say about the apostles, if Jesus himself admitted that only the Father knows the time of the end of our world, and even he, the Son of Man, does not.

About the Resurrection

What awaits a person after death? Paul was sure that those who live according to the spirit and not according to the flesh will not die but only change the form of their existence—from material to immaterial. The apostle explained to the Corinthians: "Flesh and blood cannot inherit the kingdom of God, nor does the perishable inherit the imperishable. Listen, I tell you a mystery: We will not all sleep, but we will all be changed . . . For the perishable must clothe itself with the imperishable, and the mortal with immortality" (1 Cor. 15:50–51,53). In another epistle to the Thessalonians, the apostle pursues the same thought further: "Brothers and sisters, we do not want you to be uninformed about those who sleep in death, so that you do not grieve like the rest of mankind, who have no hope. For we believe that Jesus died and rose again, and so we believe that God will bring with Jesus those who have fallen asleep in him" (1 Thess. 4:13–14). Paul, who came from the Pharisees, fully shared with them the belief in the immortality of souls, and he brought the same idea to Christianity. As for the physical resurrection of the dead after the coming of the Messiah, which was also believed by many Pharisees, from the few epistles where Paul's authorship is not disputed, it is difficult to form his true opinion. It is known that at the trial of the Sanhedrin, Paul said: "My brothers, I am a Pharisee, descended from Pharisees. I stand on trial because of the hope of the resurrection of the dead" (Acts 23:6). It is difficult to say what the apostle meant by the resurrection of the dead. It cannot be excluded that he deliberately pushed his judges against each other, knowing that some of them were Pharisees who believed in the resurrection of the dead and others were Sadducees who completely denied the possibility of such a thing.

On nonresistance to evil

Paul followed the teachings of Jesus—not to resist evil—and in his epistles he wrote, "Bless those who persecute you; bless and do not curse ... Do not repay anyone evil for evil" (Rom. 12:14,17). However, he somewhat changed this principle of Jesus, believing that the right to revenge for evil belongs not to man but to God. He urged his flock in Rome: "Do not take revenge, my dear friends, but leave room for God's wrath, for it is written: 'It is mine to avenge; I will repay,' says the Lord. On the contrary: "If your enemy is hungry, feed him; if he is thirsty, give him something to drink. In doing this, you will heap burning coals on his head" (Rom 12:19). Paul proposed not merely passive nonresistance to evil but a struggle against evil with the help of good, which should lead to vengeance on the part of the Lord himself. He wrote: "Do not be overcome by evil, but overcome evil with good" (Rom. 12:21). In this approach, there is some compromise between Old Testament morality and the teachings of Jesus. As is well known, the Old Testament principle—an eye for an eye, a tooth for a tooth—demanded adequate retribution to the offender, while Jesus excluded any revenge at all and was ready to pray for the offender so that he would not suffer punishment from God. Paul offered to avenge evil with good, leaving to the Lord the choice of punishment for the offender.

On the special role of the Jewish people in Christianity

Paul loved his people very much and was ready to make any sacrifice for their sake. He confessed: "For I could wish that I myself were cursed and cut off from Christ for the sake of my people, those of my own race, the people of Israel." According to the apostle: "Theirs is the adoption to sonship; theirs the divine glory, the covenants, the receiving of the law, the temple worship and the promises. Theirs are the patriarchs, and from them is traced the human ancestry of the Messiah, who is God over all, forever praised. Amen" (Rom. 9:3–5). Emphasizing the God-chosen Jews and their special purpose, Paul was upset that not everything happens as it should have been according to the Scriptures. And the most unexpected thing was that the Jewish people in the mass were in no hurry to accept Jesus, the Messiah who was sent to save Israel. Trying to understand this, Paul came to an important conclusion: "It is not as though God's word had failed," but that the true Israelites are not all those who call themselves by this name. "For not all who are descended from Israel are Israel. Nor because they are his descendants are they all Abraham's children . . . In other words, it is not the children by physical descent who are God's children, but it is the children of the promise who are regarded as Abraham's offspring" (Rom. 9:6–7). The true sons of Israel, according to Paul, are not just those who fulfill the commandments of God, but those whom the Lord himself considers to be such. And it is useless for a person to try to understand this, and even more so to resist his will. "But who are you, a human being, to talk back to God? "Shall what is formed say to the one who formed it, 'Why did you make me like this?'" Does not the potter have the right to make out of the same lump of clay some pottery for special purposes and some for common use?" (Rom. 9:20–21). So, not every son of Israel is the chosen one of God, but only the one who was chosen by the Lord himself. Paul recalls the words of Scripture: "I loved Jacob, but I hated Esau," and the fact that the elder (Esau) was enslaved to the younger (Jacob). But they are both twin sons of the same mother,

145

Rebekah, and the same father, the patriarch Isaac; they are both grand-sons of Abraham. Among many examples, how different can be the fate of the sons of the Jewish people, Paul quoted from Isaiah's prophecy: "Though the number of the Israelites be like the sand by the sea, only the remnant will be saved" (Rom. 9:27). This means that God's choice does not apply to the entire Jewish people, but only to a part of them, and a smaller part, and only the Lord knows who and why is among these chosen ones. Paul notes bitterly: "The Gentiles, who did not pur-sue righteousness, have obtained it, a righteousness that is by faith; but the people of Israel, who pursued the law as the way of righteous-ness, have not attained their goal. Why not? Because they pursued it not by faith but as if it were by works" (Rom 9:30–32). However, as the apostle reminds us, "Christ is the culmination of the law so that there may be righteousness for everyone who believes" (Rom 10:4). But for God "there is no difference between Jew and Gentile—the same Lord is Lord of all and richly blesses all who call on him, for, "Everyone who calls on the name of the Lord will be saved." How, then, can they call on the one they have not believed in? And how can they believe in the one of whom they have not heard?" (Rom 10:14). Here Paul comes to the most painful question for him: why most Jews have not yet accepted their own Jewish Messiah? Trying to find an explanation for this, Paul quotes the words of the prophet Isaiah, who, in conveying to Israel the will of the Lord, said: "All day long I have held out my hands to a disobe-dient and obstinate people," but "I was found by those who did not seek me; I revealed myself to those who did not ask for me" (Rom. 10:20–21). Again Paul asks himself in dismay: "Did God reject his people?" And he answers himself: "By no means! I am an Israelite myself, a descendant of Abraham, from the tribe of Benjamin. God did not reject his peo-ple, whom he foreknew" (Rom. 11:1–2). The apostle draws attention to the passage of the Scripture where the prophet Elijah complained to the Lord about his people: "Lord, they have killed your prophets and torn down your altars; I am the only one left, and they are trying to kill me." Paul finds the Lord's answer to be very significant: "I have reserved for myself seven thousand who have not bowed the knee to Baal." The apostle asserts that both in the past and present, and in all subsequent times, the Lord will surely preserve the remnant of his chosen people. These few will be chosen "by grace" and "not by works." As for the rest, their fate is unenviable, because "God gave them a spirit of stupor, eyes that could not see and ears that could not hear, to this very day" (Rom.

11:3–8). But did most of Paul's brethren "stumble so as to fall beyond recovery?" And to this question the apostle answers in the negative: "Not at all! Rather, because of their transgression, salvation has come to the Gentiles to make Israel envious. But if their transgression means riches for the world, and their loss means riches for the Gentiles, how much greater riches will their full inclusion bring!" (Rom. 11:11–12). Paul sees the will of the Lord in the fact that the majority of the Jewish people did not recognize Jesus as their Messiah, because this forced Jewish Christians to preach about Christ to other nations, and this could lead the pagan peoples to the true God.

At the same time, Paul warns Gentile converts, as well as all non-Jewish Christians in general, that the non-recognition of Jesus by the majority of Jews does not mean that they thereby deprive themselves of the status of a God-chosen people, that the Lord's covenant with them loses its validity. The Jews, "as far as election is concerned, they are loved on account of the patriarchs, for God's gifts and his call are irrevocable" (Rom. 11:28–29). Paul considers it necessary to warn Christians not to try to rise above the Jews who did not recognize Jesus, because the roots of Christianity are in Judaism, and it was the Jews who brought the gospel of Christ to other nations. The apostle reminds: "If the part of the dough offered as first fruits is holy, then the whole batch is holy; if the root is holy, so are the branches" (Rom 11:16). Paul writes to overzealous Christians and explains: "If some of the branches have been broken off, and you, though a wild olive shoot, have been grafted in among the others and now share in the nourishing sap from the olive root, do not consider yourself to be superior to those other branches. If you do, consider this: You do not support the root, but the root supports you. You will say then, "Branches were broken off so that I could be grafted in." Granted. But they were broken off because of unbelief, and you stand by faith. Do not be arrogant, but tremble. For if God did not spare the natural branches, he will not spare you either" (Rom. 11:17–21).

Paul does not want to leave Christians in the dark about the secret reason why Jews do not believe in Christ: Their rejection of Jesus is caused by the Lord himself only so that they might spread the knowledge of the true God among all the peoples of the earth. "I do not want you to be ignorant of this mystery, brothers and sisters, so that you may not be conceited: Israel has experienced a hardening in part until the full number of the Gentiles has come in, and in this way, all Israel will be saved" (Rom 11:25). In his opinion, one day all Jews will believe in their Messiah—Jesus. "After all, if you were cut out of an olive tree that is wild by nature, and contrary to nature were grafted into a cultivated olive tree, how much more readily will these, the natural branches, be grafted into their own olive tree!" (Rom. 11:24).

In singling out the Jews, Paul pointed out that they, as a people chosen for a great spiritual mission, always have a greater responsibility than others. Great honor in the good and great guilt for the bad. "There will be trouble and distress for every human being who does evil: first for the Jew, then for the Gentile; but glory, honor and peace for everyone who does good: first for the Jew, then for the Gentile" (Rom. 2:9–10). Paul asks the question: "What advantage, then, is there in being a Jew, or what value is there in circumcision?" And he answers himself: "Much in every way! First of all, the Jews have been entrusted with the very words of God" (Rom. 3:1–2). The apostle considers it necessary to support his opinion with the prophecy of Isaiah: "The Root of Jesse will spring up, one who will arise to rule over the nations; in him the Gentiles will hope" (Rom. 15:12). Paul paid attention not only to the special role of Jews in Christianity but also to the different attitudes of Jesus himself toward the Jews and the Gentiles. "For I tell you that Christ has become a servant of the Jews on behalf of God's truth, so that the promises made to the patriarchs might be confirmed, and moreover, that the Gentiles might glorify God for his mercy" (Rom. 15:8–9).

At the same time, Paul emphasized that through faith in Jesus, the differences between Jews and Gentiles, and most importantly the privilege of being a Jew, are eliminated. "Is God the God of Jews only? Is he not the God of Gentiles too? Yes, of Gentiles too, since there is only one God, who will justify the circumcised by faith and the uncircumcised through that same faith" (Rom. 3:29–30).

About circumcision

From Paul's point of view, it is not necessary for Gentiles who choose to become Christians to be circumcised, and for Jews who believe in Jesus, it is not necessary to abandon this traditional rite because circumcision itself does not change anything. "Circumcision has value if you observe the law, but if you break the law, you have become as though you had not been circumcised. So then, if those who are not circumcised keep the law's requirements, will they not be regarded as though they were circumcised? The one who is not circumcised physically and yet obeys the law will condemn you who, even though you have the written code and circumcision, are a lawbreaker. A person is not a Jew who is one only outwardly, nor is circumcision merely outward and physical. No, a person is a Jew who is one inwardly; and circumcision is circumcision of the heart, by the Spirit, not by the written code. Such a person's praise is not from other people, but from God" (Rom. 2:25–29). Paul left the question of circumcision to the discretion of the person himself. "Nevertheless, each person should live as a believer in whatever situation the Lord has assigned to them, just as God has called them. This is the rule I lay down in all the churches. Was a man already circumcised when he was called? He should not become uncircumcised. Was a man uncircumcised when he was called? He should not be circumcised. Circumcision is nothing and uncircumcision is nothing. Keeping God's commands is what counts" (1 Cor. 7:17–19). The apostle emphasizes that "for in Christ Jesus neither circumcision nor uncircumcision has any value. The only thing that counts is faith expressing itself through love" (Gal. 5:6). To confirm his words, Paul turns to the biblical story: "We have been saying that Abraham's faith was credited to him as righteousness. Under what circumstances was it credited? Was it after he was circumcised or before? It was not after, but before! And he received circumcision as a sign, a seal of the righteousness that he had by faith while he was still uncircumcised. So then, he is the father of all who believe but have not been circumcised, in order that righteousness might be credited to them" (Rom 4:9–11). If you have accepted Jesus, "in him you were also circumcised with a circumcision not performed by human hands" (Col. 2:11).

About kashrut (dietary laws)

Paul believed that new Christians who are from among the Gentiles should not be forced to follow Judaic dietary laws (kashrut), although Jewish Christians themselves could continue to observe them. Addressing first of all his fellow Jews, who were then the majority in Christian communities, the apostle urged: "Do not destroy the work of God for the sake of food . . . For the kingdom of God is not a matter of eating and drinking, but of righteousness, peace and joy in the Holy Spirit" (Rom. 14:20,17). "Eat anything sold in the meat market without raising questions of conscience, for "The earth is the Lord's, and everything in it. If an unbeliever invites you to a meal and you want to go, eat whatever is put before you without raising questions of conscience. But if someone says to you, "This has been offered in sacrifice," then do not eat it" (1 Cor. 10:25–28). From Paul's point of view, Jews who accepted Jesus were free to choose whether to observe kashrut or not. But the same right was given to Gentiles newly converted to Christianity: They were free to adhere to Jewish dietary laws or to follow their own national traditions and habits in choosing food. However, none of the members of the Christian communities were to dictate to others what was permissible to eat and what was not. Paul instructed: "The one who eats everything must not treat with contempt the one who does not, and the one who does not eat everything must not judge the one who does, for God has accepted them . . . So then, each of us will give an account of ourselves to God" (Rom. 14:3,12). At the same time, the apostle considered it necessary for new Christians from the Gentiles to observe certain Jewish prohibitions in food, such as "idolatrous" meat and carrion.

About marriage

Paul saw marriage as a necessary evil to avoid fornication. The apostle believed that in principle "it is good for a man not to have sexual relations with a woman. But since sexual immorality is occurring, each man should have sexual relations with his own wife, and each woman with her own husband" (1 Cor. 7:1–2).

> Now to the unmarried and the widows I say: It is good for them to stay unmarried, as I do. But if they cannot control themselves, they should marry, for it is better to marry than to burn with passion. To the married I give this command (not I, but the Lord): A wife must not separate from her husband. But if she does, she must remain unmarried or else be reconciled to her husband. And a husband must not divorce his wife. (1 Cor. 7:8–11)

To Christian communities, the apostle offered his view of marriage: "Are you pledged to a woman? Do not seek to be released. Are you free from such a commitment? Do not look for a wife. But if you do marry, you have not sinned; and if a virgin marries, she has not sinned. But those who marry will face many troubles in this life, and I want to spare you this" (1 Cor. 7:27–28). Paul explained his preference for celibacy as follows:

An unmarried man is concerned about the Lord's affairs—how he can please the Lord. But a married man is concerned about the affairs of this world—how he can please his wife— and his interests are divided. An unmarried woman or virgin is concerned about the Lord's affairs: Her aim is to be devoted to the Lord in both body and spirit. But a married woman is concerned about the affairs of this world—how she can please her husband. I am saying this for your own good, not to restrict you, but that you may live in a right way in undivided devotion to the Lord. (1 Cor. 7:32–34)

Convinced that the end of our world was not far off, Paul regarded marriage as a means to prevent something even worse—fornication. "The body, however, is not meant for sexual immorality but for the Lord" (1 Cor.6:13). Paul explained the need to put an end to fornication and the requirement of the indissolubility of marriage by following: "Do you not know that your bodies are temples of the Holy Spirit, who is in you, whom you have received from God? You are not your own; you were bought at a price. Therefore honor God with your bodies" (1 Cor.6:19). In his opinion, for those who have chosen to serve the Lord, it would be better to remain unmarried.

Council of Jerusalem

Preaching about Jesus outside of Judea, for example, in Syria, Cyprus, and Asia Minor, showed that Judaic laws and customs were the main obstacle to the acceptance of Christ by Gentiles. The most problematic of them was circumcision. While the Jews circumcised their sons on the eighth day after birth, when this procedure did not cause any physical complications and mental trauma, the pagans who believed in Jesus had to circumcise in adulthood, when that procedure could be painful and dangerous. The very first missionary trip of Paul and Barnabas to Cyprus and Asia Minor convinced them that without abandoning the circumcision rite, the laws of keeping the Sabbath, and kosher (dietary rules), it would not be possible to bring the pagans to the Lord. Therefore, Paul, at his own risk, even on the first trip, began to assert that faith in Jesus forgives a person for failure to comply with the laws of Judaism. Upon the return of Paul and Barnabas to Antioch, they immediately raised the issue of abandoning the requirements of circumcision, Sabbath observance, and observing the kosher laws for pagans who want to become

Christians. However, in Antioch, as in other early Christian communities, many were convinced that "unless you are circumcised, according to the custom taught by Moses, you cannot be saved" (Acts 15:1).

Disagreements between Paul and Barnabas, on the one hand, and their opponents, on the other, threatened to destroy the still fragile Christian community of Antioch. It became clear that it was impossible to resolve this problem without the authoritative opinion of Jesus's disciples and the help of the main Christian community in Jerusalem. Therefore, both sides send their messengers to Jerusalem. A meeting, which took place here, went down in history under the name of the Council of Jerusalem or Apostolic Council. This first council in the history of early Christianity took place somewhere between 49 and 51 CE. The Book of Acts is the most important source of our knowledge about this event. According to Acts, the dispute in Jerusalem was resolved by the two most reputable apostles—Peter and James (Jesus's brother), who mostly supported Paul and Barnabas. Peter was the first who had to preach among the pagans, Roman soldiers from the garrison in Caesarea, so he perfectly understood what difficulties faced by Gentiles when they join Jesus. In his defense of Paul, he put forward two main arguments. First: "God, who knows the heart, showed that he accepted them by giving the Holy Spirit to them, just as he did to us. He did not discriminate between us and them, for he purified their hearts by faith." Second, bearing in mind the difficulties in obeying all the Judaic laws, Peter believed that there is no need "to put on the necks of Gentiles a yoke that neither we nor our ancestors have been able to bear" (Acts 15:8–10). Peter was also supported by Jesus's brother, James. He reminded the call of the biblical prophets—to help other nations to find the way to the Lord. "It is my judgment, therefore, that we should not make it difficult for the Gentiles who are turning to God. Instead, we should write to them, telling them to abstain from food polluted by idols, from sexual immorality, from the meat of strangled animals and from blood" (Acts 15:19–20). But the listing of what should not be done by newly converted pagans is strangely cut off and ends with a reference to the Mosaic Law, which is read in synagogues every Saturday. Probably, the apostle James meant that pagans can get acquainted with the laws of Moses in all synagogues during the Sabbath services. The apparent cut in James's words raises the suspicion that first copyists drastically reduced the list of what Gentile Christians should avoid.

The results of the Jerusalem Council meant the triumph of Paul's idea—to free Gentiles who wanted to join Jesus from the need to perform all Jewish rites, above all circumcision. However, the victory was far from complete. As James's words indicate, pagans who decided to become Christians were required to observe not only moral but also some key dietary laws of Judaism: the prohibition against eating the meat of a dead or sick animal and against the use of any meat from which blood had not previously been removed. Peter himself demonstrated the great importance the apostles attached to these dietary laws when he arrived in Antioch and refused to eat at the same table with former pagans who did not observe these rules.

But Paul wanted more. For the sake of spreading faith in Jesus, he was ready to abandon all Jewish laws and customs, to strip Judaism of all its national features, leaving only the universal elements of Jewish monotheism. But he certainly agreed with the other apostles on one point: the basic moral principles of Judaism were to become the norms for all Christian communities. This was the beginning of the common Judeo-Christian morality of the Western world.

Paul's revolutionary idea and its consequences

While the Council of Jerusalem freed former pagans from having to fulfill most Judaic laws, notably the law mandating circumcision, nothing of the sort was done for Jewish Christians. On the contrary, the apostles— Jesus's disciples—believed that the Jews who joined Christ should continue to fully observe all the Judaic laws, traditions, and rituals. But how is it possible to bring together, as one Christian community, those who zealously observed the laws of circumcision, the Sabbath, and Kosher and ceremoniously observed Jewish holidays and those who blatantly ignored the same laws? How could a Jew who believed in Jesus and a newly converted Hellene be united? To do this, the apostle Paul took a revolutionary step—one which the apostles Peter, James, and John never accepted. By his authority, Paul freed all pagans who wanted to accept Jesus from the observance of absolutely all Judaic laws. Of all Judaism, he left for the Gentile converts only the one God of Israel, the Jewish moral that was founded on the Ten Commandments received by Moses on Mt. Sinai, and the Sacred Scripture (the Old Testament). But Paul went further: he began to claim that after the resurrection of Jesus, which proved that the latter was the true and long-awaited Jewish Messiah, there would be a kind of messianic period that will last till the end of the world and the Second Coming of Christ. During this fairly short—so the apostle thought—period, it was not necessary for former pagans to observe the Judaic laws; moreover, he believed the Jews themselves did not have to either. In Paul's view, the Mosaic laws were essential, but only before the resurrection of Christ. The apostle focused primarily not on what Jesus preached but on his resurrection. After all, Jesus's preaching was a part of the same Jewish morality that Paul had already brought to Christianity. Jesus's resurrection was the event that would radically change the fate of all humanity. In all his epistles, at least in those whose authenticity is not disputed, the apostle writes almost nothing about Jesus's life and preaching. This is no coincidence. Paul talks about what is most important for him—that is, the meaning of Jesus's resurrection for our world. "Therefore, if anyone is in Christ, the new creation has come: The old has gone, the new is here!" (2 Cor. 5:17). This was no longer religious reform; it was a real revolution in Judaism that made it possible to "Judaize" millions of Gentiles. But it now became very difficult for Jews to enter the new Judaism of Paul; to do so, they would need to give up all the features that made them Jews. Notably, Jesus's disciples, including the apostle Peter, could not do this. Thus, an unbridgeable chasm emerged between the Jewish Christians, which included all of Jesus's disciples and the Gentiles who were led by Paul to the God of Israel.

Paul's idea—to bring the masses of pagans to his simplified Jewish monotheism—did not appear by chance and by no means groundlessly. The Greco-Roman world of the first century CE was ready to accept it. The formation of the huge Roman Empire, which united within its borders many peoples who differed from one another in terms of culture and development, required a religion that would be supranational in its character. The absolute power of the emperor, a single army, and common laws for the entire empire demanded the same degree of unification and centralization in religion. The existence of numerous God-fearers among the educated Romans and Greeks testified to people's growing dissatisfaction with pagan gods and cults. And so, it was not only the political interests of the enormous empire but also the spiritual and intellectual needs of the people of that time that motivated them to turn their attention to Jewish monotheism. However, monotheism in Jewish national dress, under the burden of the difficult-to-fulfill Mosaic laws, did not have any chance of being accepted as the state religion of the entire empire. A new religion was needed—one that would rely on the idea of Jewish monotheism but would not carry any Jewish national and historical particularities. Objectively, the Greco-Roman world needed a reformer who could adapt the monotheism of the Judeans for the state and spiritual needs of the ancient world's greatest empire. And this reformer appeared. It was Paul, a man who belonged at once to two worlds—the Hellenistic and the Judean. Admittedly, there were many such people who belonged to both cultures among the Jews of that time. But Paul proved to be the one who could find the ideological justification to cut from Judaism exactly as much as was required for the Roman Empire's pagan masses. The resurrection of the Judean Messiah became the link with the help of which Paul connected Jewish monotheism to the culture of the Greco-Roman world. If Paul had not accomplished this, then it would have been done by some other Hellenized Jew who had joined Jesus's followers, such as Apollos, a Jewish religious scholar from Alexandria.

If Paul had not insisted on renouncing the Judaic laws, then his preaching of Jesus as the Messiah might have been accepted with time by the majority of Jewish people. However, in that case, only the Jews would have professed Christianity, and this religion would not have spread outside the Judean communities. But the apostle, for the sake of the Gentiles' convenience, rejected all Judaic rituals, traditions, and customs, focusing his attention on the preaching of the one God and Jesus as being the Messiah (Christ) of not only the Jewish people but of all peoples in the world. This universal, supranational idea, deprived of any Judaic features, was welcomed by the Gentiles but was unattractive to the Jews. The latter preferred that this familiar conception of the God of Israel and the Messiah be "packaged" with the just as usual Judaic laws and customs. This was also supported by the disciples of Jesus. But it was precisely this circumstance that made Judaism, in Paul's opinion, a purely national religion. The apostle, having removed everything national from Judaism, made it a universal world religion—Christianity.

There is no need to mention the enormous and positive influence that Christianity has had on the entire European civilization, which inspires in so many people feelings of gratitude and appreciation for Paul. However, Paul's brethren experienced the consequences of his revolutionary idea very differently. While the apostles lived, the Jews retained their privileged position in Christian communities. Furthermore, until the end of the first century CE, the Jews comprised the majority of these communities. But as time went on, former pagans began to prevail in terms of numbers among the Christians, and with the death of the last apostle, the Jews lost their dominant role in Christianity. Already in the first half of the second century, Gentiles replaced the Jews in the leadership of the Christian communities and took revenge for their prior humiliations on the Jews: In lieu of the spirit of reverence for the first monotheistic people in the world, there appeared a reverse tendency—enmity toward the Jews. To antisemitism, widespread among the Hellenes, the new Christian leaders added a new argument: the accusation of crucifying Jesus. But to make this reasoning more convincing, they had to edit the gospels. The copyists, with full consent of the leaders of their communities, added to the gospels anti-Jewish statements that changed the spirit and word of the original texts. Moreover, it was at this time, in the second century, that the Apocrypha appeared, in which the antisemitic sentiments of former pagans show more fully. However, since the writers of these Apocrypha never knew Christ and his apostles and did not have the slightest idea about Judean life in the time of Jesus, their forged works were rejected by the First Council of Nicaea in 325 CE.

The change in composition of Christian communities in favor of the Gentiles led to the appearance of yet another serious problem. The newly converted pagans brought to Christianity many heathen customs and views that called monotheism into question. Unlike the Jews, who came to the idea of monotheism through painful struggle against pagan cults over the course of many centuries, the Greeks, Romans, and Syrians were often unable to stay grounded in monotheism and fell into various heresies, which were, in reality, veiled forms of paganism. One of the earliest of these heresies was the Gnosticism of the Greek Marcion, which was a bizarre mix of polytheism and anti-Judaism. The apostle Paul foresaw a similar problem, and in his farewell speech to the leaders of the newly formed churches, he admitted with sadness: "I know that after I leave, savage wolves will come in among you and will not spare the flock. Even from your own number men will arise and distort the truth in order to draw away disciples after them" (Acts 20:29–30). Unfortunately, Paul's fears came true. Beginning in the second century, a strange picture emerged: the one God of Israel and his Messiah, the Jewish apostles and Mary, mother of Jesus, turned into objects of worship and veneration for the Gentiles, who, in their turn, began to persecute the people of this God and this Messiah, the descendants of the apostles and Jesus's mother.

Relationship with the disciples of Jesus

Anyone who carefully reads the epistles of Paul cannot but come to the conclusion that the apostle did not have a good relationship with the disciples of Jesus. And although the Acts try to present the relationship between the apostles as fraternal, the picture is far from perfect. Perhaps, at first, Paul was offended by the inattention and indifference of the disciples of Jesus to his far from ordinary personality and to the dramatic nature of his joining to Christ. Later, he could not help but feel that he was more educated and better prepared for missionary work than the "not bookish,"—or to put it bluntly, almost illiterate—disciples of Jesus. In turn, the disciples and former companions of Jesus could not help but resent the actions of Paul, who by his own power abolished the laws of Moses for the Jews, which was unthinkable during the earthly life of Christ. To the disciples of Jesus and their entourage, Paul was an impostor who not only never knew Christ, but also did not want to honor his followers. For his part, Paul made no secret of the fact that he did not bow down to any of the apostles, even to those who were the closest associates of Jesus. "As for those who were held in high esteem—whatever they were makes no difference to me; God does not show favoritism—they added nothing to my message" (Gal. 2:6).

Paul was sincerely convinced that he was doing incomparably more for the gospel of Jesus than all his disciples. Responding to his highly respected critics from among the apostles, Paul wrote:

Are they Hebrews? So am I. Are they Israelites? So am I. Are they Abraham's descendants? So am I. Are they servants of Christ? (I am out of my mind to talk like this.) I am more. I have worked much harder, been in prison more frequently, been flogged more severely, and been exposed to death again and again . . . Three times I was beaten with rods, once I was pelted with stones, three times I was shipwrecked, I spent a night and a day in the open sea, I have been constantly on the move. I have been in danger from rivers, in danger from bandits, in danger from my fellow Jews, in danger from Gentiles; in danger in the city, in danger in the country, in danger at sea; and in danger from false believers. I have labored and toiled and have often gone without sleep; I have known hunger and thirst and have often gone without food; I have been cold and naked. (2 Cor. 11:22–23,25–27)

However, the relationship between Paul and the disciples of Jesus was not always bad. Thus, fourteen years after his first visit, Paul, together with Barnabas and Titus, a Greek by birth, again came to Jerusalem to discuss with the apostles Peter, John, and James the missionary work among the Gentiles. Then the apostles approved this idea. Paul himself writes about this as follows: "James, Cephas and John, those esteemed as pillars, gave me and Barnabas the right hand of fellowship when they recognized the grace given to me. They agreed that we should go to the Gentiles, and they to the circumcised" (Gal. 2:9).

Saint Peter and Saint Paul. Painting by El Greco, 1587-1592.

However, much more characteristic were the conflicts, one of which Paul recalls in his epistle to the Galatians. This encounter took place between him and the apostle Peter, who had come to Antioch to meet the newly converted Christians from the Gentiles. Initially, when Peter shared meals with them, he did not require them to observe kashrut, but later, when a group of Jewish Christians sent by James (Jesus's brother) arrived from Jerusalem to Antioch, Peter stopped eating with those who did not observe kashrut. Paul himself writes the following about the quarrel with Peter:

> When Cephas came to Antioch, I opposed him to his face, because he stood condemned. For before certain men came from James, he used to eat with the Gentiles. But when they arrived, he began to draw back and separate himself from the Gentiles because he was afraid of those who belonged to the circumcision group. The other Jews joined him in his hypocrisy, so that by their hypocrisy even Barnabas was led astray. When I saw that they were not acting in line with the truth of the gospel, I said to Cephas in front of them all, "You are a Jew, yet you live like a Gentile and not like a Jew. How is it, then, that you force Gentiles to follow Jewish customs?" (Gal. 2:11–14)

In fact, the conflict between Paul and Peter had more serious roots than the disagreement over the observance of kashrut at the joint meals of Jewish Christians and Gentile converts. We must not forget that the Council of Jerusalem was, in fact, a shaky compromise between the positions of Paul, on the one hand, and the disciples of Jesus, on the other. The Council exempted Gentile converts from the observance of most of the Judaic laws, but it did not abolish any of them for the Jews themselves. But Paul called not only the Gentiles but also the Jews to abandon all the laws of Judaism because they were to be replaced by faith in the risen Jesus. If Paul preached essentially a new religion, then the disciples of Jesus remained rooted in traditional Judaism. The differences were fundamental and would eventually lead to a real ideological war. The alienation also affected the apostles' associates; for example, Barnabas always stood on the side of Paul, but his nephew John Mark (the author of the Gospel of Mark) was close to Peter, which is why Paul refused to take him on a second missionary trip. However, the martyrdom of the apostles at the hands of Roman pagans reconciled both sides and hid the nature of their conflict for posterity.

The long way to Roman Calvary

Upon his return to Jerusalem from his third missionary trip, Paul's situation became seriously complicated. The apostle was blamed for convincing not only the Gentiles but also the Jews themselves not to fulfill the laws of Judaism if they believed in Jesus. From the point of view of many members of the Christian community, this was a violation of the decisions of the Jerusalem Council, which exempted only Gentile converts, but not the Jews themselves, from observing the Law of Moses. The leaders of the Jerusalem church also felt that Paul had gone too far, and James, Jesus's brother, made it clear to him, albeit in a gentle, tactful way. James asked Paul to refute before the entire Christian community the claims that he was teaching all Jews living among the Gentiles "to turn away from Moses, telling them not to circumcise their children or live according to our customs" (Acts 21:21). The leaders of the church in Jerusalem urged Paul to abandon what he had called the Jews of Asia Minor and Greece to do. "Then everyone will know there is no truth in these reports about you, but that you yourself are living in obedience to the law" (Acts 21:24). The Church of Jerusalem had good reasons for this position. The preaching among the Jews that faith in Jesus made it unnecessary to observe the Mosaic Law was doomed to failure in Judea. And Jesus himself never called on the Jews to abandon the Law of Moses. What the pagan Gentiles needed was not acceptable to the monotheistic Jews. This was the main problem of Paul's sermons. However, in personal terms, it was easy for Paul, as a devout Jew, to find a common language with the Jerusalem church. Although Paul claimed that faith in Jesus allows people not to observe the laws of Judaism, he always tried to fulfill them. For example, he celebrated Passover, inviting even non-Jews to it, and usually interrupted his missionary trips to make a pilgrimage to Jerusalem on the main Jewish holidays, in particular, on Shavuot (Pentecost) (Acts 20:16).

If the dissatisfaction of the Jewish Christians was mitigated by the advocacy of James, the recognized moral leader of the Jerusalem community, then the indignation of the Jews from Asia Minor and Greece, where Paul actually preached, threatened serious trouble. As Paul's friends had feared, the pilgrims from Asia Minor burned with anger when they saw the apostle in the Temple. "They stirred up the whole crowd and seized him, shouting, "Fellow Israelites, help us! This is the man who teaches everyone everywhere against our people and our law and this place" (Acts 21:27–28). The riots in the Temple attracted the attention of Roman soldiers, who arrested Paul and took him to the fortress of Antonia, which was located directly opposite the Temple complex. All the attempts of the apostle to explain himself from the fortress to the inhabitants of Jerusalem also came to nothing because the pilgrims from Asia Minor, who remembered his sermons well, "were shouting and throwing off their cloaks and flinging dust into the air" (Acts 22:23). The commander of the Roman garrison, Claudius Lysias, fearing that the indignation of the crowd would turn into anti-Roman riots, hastened to take Paul to the interior of the fortress for questioning. However, the proceedings further complicated the case. It turned out that Paul was a Roman citizen, so he should have been judged only by the Romans, not by the Jews. Then Claudius Lysias, wanting to understand the charges against the prisoner, demanded that the Sanhedrin convene.

Paul understood that the Sanhedrin had no real power over him, a Roman citizen, a native of the Cilician city of Tarsus, but decided to confuse and push his judges against each other. Knowing that the members of the court were actually split into two opposing factions, the Sadducees and the Pharisees, he reminded them both of his Pharisaic background and of his Pharisaic views. He

> called out in the Sanhedrin, "My brothers, I am a Pharisee, the son of a Pharisee. I stand on trial because of the hope in the resurrection of the dead." When he said this, a dispute broke out between the Pharisees and the Sadducees, and the assembly was divided. The Sadducees say that there is no resurrection, and that there are neither angels nor spirits, but the Pharisees acknowledge them all). There was a great uproar, and some of the teachers of the law who were Pharisees stood up and argued vigorously. "We find nothing wrong with this man," they said. "What if a spirit or an angel has spoken to him?" (Acts 23:6–9)

Fortunately for Paul, his opponents, who came from Asia Minor, were not represented in the Sanhedrin, and the most dangerous accusation, that he willfully freed the Jews from the need to fulfill the laws of Moses, was never heard in court. Disappointed by the outcome of the Sanhedrin, the Romans sent Paul back to the fortress of Antonia. However, the apostle's position remained precarious. If the Jews of Jerusalem did not know Paul and did not harbor any hostile intentions toward him, the same could not be said of the pilgrims from Asia

Minor. They were burning with indignation and could insist on a second convocation of the Sanhedrin, whose outcome would be difficult to predict. In any case, if a Roman trial was inevitable, it should not have been burdened with the authoritative opinion of the Sanhedrin. Therefore, the Jewish Christians of Jerusalem and the friends of the apostle believed that it would be better for Paul to appear just before the Roman court. Paul himself was inclined to the same opinion. As the case of proconsul Gallio of Achaia (Greece) showed, the Romans do not interfere in theological disputes between Jews, so all charges against Paul would be dropped by them. Wanting to help Paul, the local Jewish Christians convinced Claudius Lysias that pilgrims from Asia Minor might attempt to kill the prisoner in Jerusalem, so he should be sent to a safer place—to Caesarea, to the Roman procurator Felix. The commander of the Roman garrison himself wanted to get rid of a man whose presence could stir up an already restless city. If, from the point of view of the law, Paul could not avoid the Roman court, then why not speed the process up?

The Acts contains the text of a report from Claudius Lysias to the procurator Felix about the transfer of Paul to Caesarea. It seems highly doubtful that such a letter could have passed from the Roman archive two decades after the events into the hands of Luke, the alleged author of the Acts and the Gospel of Luke. Obviously, like some other parts of the text of the Acts, it was added after Luke's death by first copyists of the New Testament. The content of the letter explains in the best way the reason for its inclusion in the text of the Acts. In the so-called report, the Jews are accused of all sins, and the Romans are exposed as the guardians and defenders of Christians. The content of the letter indicates that the copyist from the converted pagans did not know the specifics of the reports in the Roman army at that time, so he composed it in the form of an ordinary letter (Acts 23:26–30).

The next stage in Paul's odyssey was the trial at the residence of Felix, the Roman governor in Judea. This time Paul was accused only of stirring up trouble among the Jews from the Diaspora by his heresy and of desecrating the Temple by bringing the Gentiles there (Acts 24:5–6). But the apostle strongly denied this and emphasized that his "Nazarene heresy" fully corresponds to the Scriptures and the beliefs of his accusers. Seeing that the essence of Paul's "transgressions" concerned the interpretation of the laws of Judaism, Felix decided to postpone the case indefinitely, leaving the apostle under house arrest in Caesarea. Being more a diplomat than a military man, the Roman procurator preferred to act on the principle that the wolves were fed and the sheep were safe. By removing Paul from Jerusalem and denying him the opportunity to preach in the Diaspora, he also created normal conditions for him to live in Caesarea. The political situation in Judea and Rome should have prompted further actions.

The uncertainty in Paul's position in Caesarea continued for two years until Felix was succeeded by a new Roman procurator in Judea, Porcius Festus (59–62). Being convinced that the charges against the apostle were mainly theological in nature, Festus invited him to go with him to Jerusalem, where the Sanhedrin would meet under the presidency of the Roman procurator. However, Paul, unsure of the outcome of the proceedings in the Sanhedrin, continued to insist on a purely Roman trial before the emperor himself, to which he was entitled as a Roman citizen. Paul's desire was in line with the interests of both the Roman procurator and the high priest of the Temple in Jerusalem; neither of them wanted to add unnecessary agitation to the already heated atmosphere of Jerusalem. And the opponents of the apostle, who came from Asia Minor, as he did, were also mostly Roman citizens and had no direct relation to Judea and Jerusalem. The courtesy visit of the Judean king Agrippa II to Caesarea strengthened Festus's opinion that Paul should be sent to Rome for the emperor's trial. "Agrippa said to Festus, "This man could have been set free if he had not appealed to Caesar" (Acts 26:32). Thus happened the fatal turn in the fate of Paul. Neither he nor his associates and friends could have imagined that the judgment of the Roman Emperor Nero would be much more terrible than any decision of the Judean Sanhedrin.

Paul's journey to Rome did not begin at a good hour. We don't know exactly what year it happened, probably around 60 CE, but we do know that the ship sailed at the end of summer, when sailing the Mediterranean becomes risky. Obviously, the centurion Julius, who was responsible for delivering Paul and the other prisoners to Rome, expected to reach Italy before winter, when the voyage is considered very dangerous. Paul boarded the ship together with his friend and assistant Luke, to whom we owe a detailed description of this journey. Only the first part of the path, from Caesarea in Judea to Sidon in Phoenicia, was pleasant and easy. But then the problems started. Due to a strong headwind, it was not possible to sail along the Syrian coast—the ship drifted to Cyprus. Because of the same wind, the ship was able to approach the shore of Asia Minor only in the area of Lycia. Here in the Lycian Myra, a Roman centurion decided to transfer all prisoners to a larger ship that was carrying wheat from Alexandria to Rome. But again, because of the unfavorable wind, the voyage was greatly delayed. The ship reached the island of Crete too late, after autumn had arrived. In Acts, Luke notes with alarm: "Much time had been lost, and sailing had already become dangerous because by now it was after the Day of Atonement. So Paul warned them, "Men, I can see that our voyage is going to be disastrous and bring great loss to ship and cargo, and to our own lives also." But the centurion, instead of listening to what Paul said, followed the advice of the pilot and of the owner of the ship. Since the harbor was unsuitable to winter in, the majority decided that we should sail on, hoping to reach Phoenix and winter there. This was a harbor in Crete, facing both southwest and northwest" (Acts 27:9–12). The Cretan port of Phoenix was considered a suitable place to leave a ship for the winter. But in order to reach this port, the ship had to go out to sea again. Suddenly the favorable south wind changed, "the ship was caught by the storm and could not head into the wind; so we gave way to it and were driven along" (Acts 27:15). Luke, Paul's companion in misfortune, describes the situation as follows: "When neither sun nor stars appeared for many days and the storm continued raging, we finally gave up all hope of being saved . . . On the fourteenth night we were still being driven across the Adriatic Sea, when about midnight the sailors sensed they were approaching land" (Acts 27:20,27). To lighten the ship as much as possible, it was necessary to throw overboard not only the entire cargo of wheat, but even the personal belongings of passengers and crew. Finally, in the light of day, the shore appeared, to which they decided to dock.

> But the ship struck a sandbar and ran aground. The bow stuck fast and would not move, and the stern was broken to pieces by the pounding of the surf. The soldiers planned to kill the prisoners to prevent any of them from swimming away and escaping. But the centurion wanted to spare Paul's life and kept them from carrying out their plan. He ordered those who could swim to jump overboard first and get to land. The rest were to get there on planks or on other pieces of the ship. In this way everyone reached land safely. (Acts 27:41–44)

The typical merchant ship in the first century CE.
Relief from the mausoleum in Pompeii, Italy.

All 276 souls who were on the ship were saved.

The land to which the travelers had come with such adventures turned out to be the island of Malta, which was under the rule of Rome. Local residents warmly welcomed the castaways, and the Roman administration of the island also provided assistance. After wintering in Malta, Paul, along with other prisoners and passengers, was put on another Alexandrian ship, which sailed to southern Italy via Sicily. This time they managed to travel without adventures. After a three-day stay in Syracuse (Sicily), the ship set sail and arrived at Rhegium, south of the Apennine peninsula. The next day, the south wind came up, and on the following day, the travelers reached Puteoli. Here Paul met his fellow Jews, who invited all the travelers to spend a whole week with them. From Puteoli, all the passengers and the prisoners with their guards had to go to Rome on foot. But in Rome, after a difficult journey, Paul had a pleasant meeting: all the local Jews, along with those who had accepted Jesus, went out to greet the famous prisoner. It is noteworthy that long before Paul's arrival in Rome, there were already heated debates among Jews about how to perceive Jesus. This controversy so inflamed the situation in the capital of the empire that the emperor Claudius, losing all patience, demanded that all disputants, both supporters and opponents of Jesus, be removed from the city. It was then that the Jewish spouses Aquila and Priscila, who had become Paul's assistants, were forced to leave Rome (Acts 28:22).

Three days later, Paul called together the local Jewish leaders. When they had assembled, Paul said to them: "I have done nothing against our people or against the customs of our ancestors . . . I was compelled to make an appeal to Caesar. I certainly did not intend to bring any charge against my own people. For this reason I have asked to see you and talk with you. It is because of the hope of Israel that I am bound with this chain" (Acts 28:17,19–20). Acts concludes its account of Paul with the following sentence: "For two whole years Paul stayed there in his own rented house and welcomed all who came to see him. He proclaimed the kingdom of God and taught about the Lord Jesus Christ—with all boldness and without hindrance!" (Acts 28:30–31). However, the evangelist Luke, a friend and colleague of Paul, must have known about the last years of his life, especially since the Acts were written 15–20 years after apostle's tragic death. We have every reason to believe that the last part of this New Testament work was intentionally never written so as not to write about the brutal executions of the first Christians by Romans.

Our information about Paul's subsequent fate in Rome is very contradictory. According to one version, after two years of house arrest, the apostle was released and, taking advantage of his freedom, realized his lifelong dream—he visited Spain, where he preached to the pagans. Some biblical scholars believe that his complete release was made possible by the intercession of envoys from Judea, among them the future historian Flavius Josephus. It is possible that the wife of Emperor Nero, Poppaea Sabina, who converted to Judaism, also took part in the fate of the apostle. However, there is another, much more reliable version, according to which, after a short liberty, Paul was again arrested and this time put not under house arrest, but in a Roman prison, where the conditions of his detention were incomparably worse than before. In the mid-'60s, Emperor Nero decided to blame the fire in Rome on Christians, and all Roman Christians, then mostly Jews, were subjected to reprisals and painful executions. Their leader, Paul, did not escape this fate. By order of Nero, he was beheaded, most likely between 64 and 67 CE

Paul's Epistles: Authentic and Attributed

Among the 27 works that make up the officially recognized canon of the New Testament, 14 are Pauline epistles. They also represent the earliest parts of the New Testament and were written by the apostle from the late 40s to the mid—60s, that is, before the creation of the four canonical gospels. However, only seven of Paul's epistles were actually written by the apostle himself. Paul's original letters include 1 and 2 Corinthians, Galatians, Philippians, Romans, Philemon, and finally 1 Thessalonians. As for the second half of Paul's epistles, there is complete consensus among biblical scholars that they were written a century after Paul's death and signed with his name to sanctify them with the authority of the most respected apostle. The epistles attributed to Paul include Colossians, Ephesians, Hebrews, 2 Thessalonians, and three so-called "pastoral" epistles: 1 and 2 Timothy and Titus. In terms of their vocabulary, style, and Church issues they discuss, none of these letters have anything to do with Paul.

The best example of how Paul's letters were falsified retroactively is the epistle to Titus, the apostle's assistant. First, Paul never sent Titus to Crete, which the real author of the letter should have known. Second, the church depicted in this epistle was incomparably more established and developed than it was in the time of Paul in the middle of the first century. Third, the vocabulary and style of this letter are completely inconsistent with the original Pauline epistles. Fourth, Paul, as an apostle of the Gentiles, would never have allowed himself to write a blatant slander against the Cretans: "Cretans are always liars, evil brutes, lazy gluttons" (Titus 1:12). Finally, the apostle, as a true Jew, could never have written the following words: "pay no attention to Jewish myths." On the contrary, he was very attentive to these "myths," and he argued his beliefs according to them. (Titus 1:14). This epistle ascribed to the apostle only occasionally has phrases written by Paul, which were taken from his other, authentic letters. (Judging by the style and vocabulary, the author of the epistle to Titus was also the author of two other "pastoral" works—the 1st and 2nd letters to Timothy.) Although half of Paul's epistles were not actually written by him, we cannot disregard them. Even if they are a century younger than the apostle and do not belong to his pen, these epistles are also historical records from the early Christian Church of the second century.

It must be noted that even the original Pauline epistles did not avoid some of the insertions and additions made by the copyists of the New

Testament writings. An example is Paul's 1 Thessalonians. Here, to the words of the apostle who praises the newly converted Gentiles for having succeeded in creating the same Christian communities as the Jewish Christians in Judea, an antisemitic insert was added. Paul writes as follows: "For you, brothers and sisters, became imitators of God's churches in Judea, which are in Christ Jesus." Then an unknown second—century copyist inserts his own continuation: "You suffered from your own people the same things those churches suffered from the Jews who killed the Lord Jesus and the prophets and also drove us out. They displease God and are hostile to everyone in their effort to keep us from speaking to the Gentiles so that they may be saved. In this way they always heap up their sins to the limit. The wrath of God has come upon them at last" (1 Thess. 2:14–16). These words are a later insertion by an anti-Jewish copyist, probably a former pagan from the Hellenes. The insertion is inappropriate and clearly does not correspond to the previous words of Paul. One can imagine what Paul's reaction would have been if he had known what those to whom he preached about Jesus would do to his messages.

Other distortions of the original Pauline epistles are related to anti-feminism. In 1 Corinthians, to the apostle is attributed the following opinion on the role of women in the Church: "Women should remain silent in the churches. They are not allowed to speak, but must be in submission, as the law says. If they want to inquire about something, they should ask their own husbands at home; for it is disgraceful for a woman to speak in the church" (1 Cor. 14:34–35). The above quotation, although artfully inserted in the original text of the epistle, does not really correspond to the apostle's views on the role of women. Paul was convinced that "there is neither male nor female, for you are all one in Christ Jesus" (Gal.3:28). He assigned the same status to men and women in Christ. In his epistle to Romans, he writes: "I commend to you our sister Phoebe, a deacon of the church in Cenchreae. I ask you to receive her in the Lord in a way worthy of his people and to give her any help she may need from you, for she has been the benefactor of many people, including me" (Rom. 16:1–2). The apostle mentions other women who were not silent, but played an important role in the development of the Church. All these additions and insertions were put into Paul's epistles in the second century, when, with impunity, copyists edited the New Testament writings according to their views.

We must not forget that in addition to the canonical New Testament works connected to Paul—the 14 epistles and the Acts of the Holy

Apostles—there are extensive apocryphal writings about the apostle of the Gentiles. Almost a dozen apocrypha dedicated to Paul have come down to our time: Acts of Peter and Paul, Acts of Paul, Acts of Paul and Thecla, The Martyrdom of the Holy Apostle Paul, Letters of Paul and Seneca, Third Epistle to the Corinthians, Apocalypse of Paul, Epistle to the Laodiceans (this letter is lost). From the 2nd to the 5th centuries, there were at least a hundred such apocrypha. All of them, without exception, are outright fakes, composed by former pagans. Even in the early centuries of our era, the Church fathers rejected almost all of this "literature" as false or unreliable, having nothing to do with the historical Paul. Today's biblical studies unequivocally confirm this verdict.

Epilogue

BEFORE THE DESTRUCTION OF Jerusalem in 70 CE, Christianity was just one of the trends of Judaism. It existed in its so-called Petrine form and differed from other currents of Judaism only by recognizing Jesus as the Messiah—the messenger of the Lord and Savior of the Jewish people. At that time, the Christian communities of both Judea and the Greco-Roman world consisted exclusively of Jews and those Gentiles (God-worshippers) who had almost converted to Judaism. It is not surprising that the first Christians prayed in the same synagogues as the rest of the Jews, and in Jerusalem, they preached in the Temple itself. Other religious movements (Pharisees, Sadducees, Essenes) looked at Christianity as another legitimate stream of Judaism. It is noteworthy that the high priest's execution of the apostle James (the brother of Jesus) in 62 CE was of an exclusively personal nature and was unanimously condemned by all the spiritual leaders of Judaism. The conversion of pagans to Christianity was not yet widespread, so Gentile converts were not exempt from all the laws of Judaism but only from the need for circumcision and compliance with the rules of kashrut.

However, the Great Jewish Revolt against the Roman Empire (66–73), the destruction of Jerusalem and its Temple, and the death or captivity of almost a million Jews radically changed the course of the development of Christianity. During the fierce battles in Galilee and the siege of Jerusalem, the Romans killed most of the Jewish Christians. Only a few of them, who escaped to Pella, one of the Hellenistic cities of the Decapolis in the Transjordan region, survived. The sharp weakening of the most authoritative Church of Jerusalem, as well as the severe consequences of the first Jewish-Roman War, marked the beginning of the separation of Christianity from Judaism. The Roman authorities stripped the Jews of all the privileges they had enjoyed before the war and even imposed additional taxes and restrictions on them. According to the decree of Emperor Vespasian, the donations collected annually for the

Temple of the Lord in Jerusalem were now to go to the pagan temple of Jupiter Capitolinus in Rome. Frightened by the scale of the Great Revolt, the Romans forbade the Jews not only to rebuild Jerusalem but even to settle on its land. This repressive policy dramatically accelerated the separation of Christianity from Judaism. Christian communities, which did not want to fall under all these restrictions and taxes, hastened to declare their independence from Judaism. If we wanted to name the exact time of the break between Judaism and Christianity, we could say it was the end of the first century. It is then that the Roman authorities begin to clearly separate Jews and Christians. For example, in 96 CE, the Emperor Nerva, unlike his predecessor Domitian, imposed an additional tax only on those who practice Judaism (both Jews and converted Gentiles) but exempted Christians (both Jews and Gentiles) from it.

The devastation of Judea caused irreparable damage not only to the Church of Jerusalem but also to the Petrine version of Christianity that dominated there. After the Jewish War, the center of influence within Christendom moved from Jerusalem to Rome and Greece, where the communities consisted mainly of former pagans who held a Pauline version of Christianity. Unlike the disciples of Jesus, who did not go beyond the borders of Judaism, Paul's followers in Italy, Greece, and Asia Minor, on the contrary, sought to leave Judaism, in which they felt like strangers. The second Jewish-Roman War—the Bar Kokhba rebellion (132–135 CE)—completed the separation of the two religions. Again, the main motivation for this was the new wave of anti-Judaism that followed the suppression of the uprising. Emperor Hadrian, trying to force all people to forget even the name of the country of the Jews, changed the name Judea to Palestine, and on the site of the destroyed Jerusalem built the new Hellenistic city of Elia Capitolina. Moreover, he forbade Jews to live on the site of their capital--and everywhere else across Judea. The emperor's new anti-Jewish edicts force Christians to accelerate their complete separation from Judaism. So, in order not to look like Jews in the eyes of the vengeful Romans, Christians do not make Saturday a day of rest but Sunday, though Christ himself and his disciples celebrated the Sabbath. However, the hasty separation from the Jews brought Christians only temporary relief. When the period of Jewish revolts and, consequently, anti-Jewish persecution ended, the Roman authorities, leaving the Jews alone, fell with all their force on the Christians as the main enemies of the empire.

The separation of Christianity from Judaism gave rise to active anti-Jewish rhetoric among the apologists of the new religion. This phenomenon was forced, since the early Church fathers had to explain to their flock how Christianity differs from Judaism and why it is better than the latter. After all, most of the biblical books (the entire Old Testament), morality, and most importantly, the one God-Father were borrowed from Judaism. The spiritual leaders of the new religion tried to convince the members of their communities that they, Christians, were the "New Israel" with which, according to the prophecy of Isaiah, a New Covenant should be concluded. Therefore, God's favor and the entire spiritual heritage of the Jews should pass to them, the Christians. But to prove all this, it was necessary to discredit Judaism and explain that after the coming of Christ, the laws of Judaism lost their meaning. In this, Paul's argument played a major role, although the apostle himself warned that the Jews' non-recognition of Christ did not mean that they were thereby deprived of the status of a God-chosen people or that the Lord's covenant with them had lost its force (Rom.11:16,28–29). Another reason for the anti-Judaism of the early Church was the desire to attract to Christianity those pagans who hesitated in their choice between two religions with an identical spiritual heritage.

It is noteworthy that in the first two centuries of Christianity's existence as an independent religion, Jewish spiritual leaders did not pay any attention to the anti-Judean rhetoric of the Church fathers. They were incomparably more concerned with the idolatry of the peoples around them as well as their own schismatics—Jewish Christians. It was the latter, known in Christianity as the Ebionites, who aroused the greatest concern and criticism of Rabbinic Judaism. The Ebionites have considered themselves the direct heirs of the Church of Jerusalem and adhered to the Petrine version of Christianity. They traced their origins to those members of the Jerusalem church who had managed to escape to Hellenistic Pella shortly before the Roman siege of Jerusalem. The rabbis called them heretics (*minim*) and regularly cursed them in an especially composed prayer (*birkat ha-minim*). As for Gentile Christians, they were of no interest to Judaism at that time; at least in the Mishnah, created in the 2nd to 3rd centuries, they are scarcely mentioned. The situation changed only in the 4th century, when Christianity became the state religion of the Roman Empire—but these events are beyond the scope of this book.

Selected Bibliography

Allison, D.C. *Jesus of Nazareth: Millenarian Prophet*. Fortress, Minneapolis, 1998.

Anderson, Paul N., Just, Felix, and Thatcher, Tom, eds. *John, Jesus, and History: Aspects of Historicity in the Fourth Gospel*. Vol. 2. Atlanta: Society of Biblical Literature, 2009.

Apostolic Fathers. A New Translation by Rick Brannan. Bellingham WA: Lexham Press, 2017

Borg, M.J. *A New Vision: Spirit, Culture and Discipleship*. San-Francisco: HarperSan-Francisco, 1987.

Brandon, S.G.F. *Jesus and the Zealots*. New York: Charles Scribner's Sons, 1967.

Broadhead, E.K. *Jewish Ways of Following Jesus: Redrawing the Religious Map of Antiquity*. Tubingen: Mohr Siebeck, 2010.

Brown, R.E. *The Birth of the Messiah*. New York: Doubleday, 1999.

Casey, Maurice. *Is John's Gospel True?* New York: Routledge, 1996.

Charlesworth, J.H. *Jesus within Judaism*. London: SPCK, 1989.

Charlesworth, J.H. (ed.), *Jesus' Jewishness: Exploring the place of Jesus in Early Judaism*. New York: Crossroad, 1991.

Chilton, Bruce. *Rabbi Jesus: An Intimate Biography*. New York: Doubleday, 2000.

Cohen, Shaye J.D. *The Beginnings of Jewishness*. University of California, 1999.

Collins, A.Y. and Collins J.J. *King and Messiah as Son of God*. Grand Rapids: Eerdmans, 2008.

Crossan, J.D. *The Historical Jesus: The Life of a Mediterranean Jewish Peasant*. San Francisco: HarperSanFrancisco, 1991.

Crossan, J.D. *Who killed Jesus? Exposing the Roots of Anti-Semitism in the Gospel Story of the Death of Jesus*. San Francisco: HarperCollins, 1998.

Crossan, John D. and Reed, Jonathan. *In Search of Paul*, Harper SanFrancisco, 2004.

Crossley, James G. *The Date of Mark's Gospel: Insight from the Law in Earliest Christianity.* London: T&T Clark, 2004.

Dunn, James D.G. *Beginning from Jerusalem.* Grand Rapids: Eerdmans, 2009.

Dunn, James D.G. *The Partings of the ways between Christianity and Judaism.* SCM, 2006.

Ehrman, Bart D. *Forged: Writing in the Name of God: Why the Bible's Authors Are Not Who We Think They Are.* New York: HarperOne, 2011.

Ehrman, Bart D. *Jesus before the Gospels: How the Earliest Christians Remembered, Changed, and Invented Their Stories of the Savior.* New York: HarperOne, 2016.

Ehrman, Bart D. *The New Testament: A Historical Introduction to Early Christian Writings.* 6th ed. Oxford: Oxford University Press, 2016.

Eusebius. *The History of the Church from Christ to Constantine.* Trans. G.A. Williamson, Rev. and ed. Andrew Louth. New York: Penguin Books, 1989.

Flusser, David. *Judaism and the Origins of Christianity.* Jerusalem: Magness Press, 1988.

Fredriksen, Paula. *From Jesus to Christ: The Origins of the New Testament Images of Christ.* 2nd ed. Yale University Press, 2000.

Fredriksen, Paula. *When Christians were Jews. The First Generation.* New Haven: Yale University Press, 2018.

Funk, Robert W. *The Five Gospels: The Search for the Authentic Words of Jesus,* HarperCollins, 1993.

Gruen, Erich S. *Diaspora: Jews amidst Greeks and Romans.* Cambridge, MA: Harvard University Press, 2009.

Hahn, F. *The Titles of Jesus in Christology.* Cambridge: Lutterworth Press, 1969.

Harrill, J. Albert. *Paul the Apostle: His Life and Legacy in Their Roman Context.* Cambridge: Cambridge University Press, 2012.

Hengel, Martin. *Between Jesus and Paul.* Philadelphia: Fortress Press, 1983.

Hengel, M. *The Son of God: The Origin of Christology and the History of Jewish-Hellenistic Religion.* London: SCM, 1976.

Horsley, Richard A. *Jesus and the Politics of Roman Palestine.* Columbia: University of South Carolina Press, 2014.

Jackson-McCabe, Matt A. *Jewish Christianity Reconsidered* (ed.). Fortress Press, 2007.

Juel, Donald H. Messianic Exegesis: *Christological Interpretation of the Old Testament in Early Christianity.* Philadelphia: Fortress Press, 1988.

King, Karen L. *What Is Gnosticism?* Cambridge, MA: Belknap Press of Harvard University Press, 2003.

Kloppenborg, John S. *Excavating Q: The History and Setting of the Sayings Gospel.* Minneapolis: Fortress Press, 2000.

Kloppenborg, John S. *Q, the Earliest Gospel: An Introduction to the Original Stories and Sayings of Jesus.* Louisville: Westminster John Knox, 2008.

Kraemer, Ross Shepard. *Unreliable Witnesses: Religion, Gender, and History in the Greco-Roman Mediterranean.* New York: Oxford University Press, 2011.

Kraft, Robert A. *Exploring the Scripturesque: Jewish Texts and Their Christian Contexts.* Brill, 2009.

Lee, B.J. *The Galilean Jewishness of Jesus: Retrieving of Jewish Origins of Christianity.* New York: Paulist Press, 1988.

Litwa, M. David. *Iesus Deus: The Early Christian Depiction of Jesus as a Mediterranean God.* Minneapolis: Fortress Press, 2014.

Mason, Steve. *Josephus and the New Testament.* 2nd ed. Grand Rapids: Baker Academic Publishing, 2003.

Metzger, Bruce M. *The Canon of the New Testament: Its Origin, Development, and Significance.* Oxford: Clarendon Press, 1987.

New Testament Apocrypha. Ed. and trans. E. Hennecke and W. Schneemelcher. 2 vols. Philadelphia: Westminster Press, 1963-64.

Nirenberg, David. *Anti-Judaism. The Western Tradition.* New York: W.W. Norton, 2013.

Novenson, Matthew. *Christ among the Messiahs.* New York: Oxford University Press, 2012.

Otto, R. *The Kingdom of God and the Son of Man.* Cambridge: James Clarke, 2010.

Reed, Annette Y. *Jewish Christianity and the History of Judaism.* Tubingen: Mohr Siebeck, 2017.

Robbins, Vernon K. *Jesus the Teacher: A Socio-Rhetorical Interpretation of Mark.* Minneapolis: Fortress Press, 1992.

Saldarini, Anthony J. "Reading Matthew without Anti-Semitism." In: *The Gospel of Matthew in Current Study: Studies in Memory of William G. Thompson,* edited by Aune, David E., 166–84. Grand Rapids: Eerdmans, 2001.

Sanders, E.P. *Jesus and Judaism.* London: SCM, 1985.

Sanders, E.P. *Paul: The Apostle's Life, Letters and Thought.* Minneapolis: Fortress Press, 2015.

Schweitzer, A. *The Quest of the Historical Jesus.* London: SCM, 2000.

Smallwood, E. Mary. *The Jews under Roman Rule: From Pompey to Diocletian: A Study in Political Relations.* Boston: Brill, 2001.

Taylor, J.E. *The Immerser: John the Baptist within Second Temple Judaism.* Grand Rapids: Eerdmans, 1997.

Tertullian. *On the Flesh of Christ.* Ed. and Trans.by Ernest Evans. London: SPCK, 1956.

Theissen, Gerd. *The Religion of the Earliest Churches: Creating a Symbolic World.* Translated by Bowden, John. Minneapolis: Fortress Press, 1999.

Thiessen, Matthew. *Contesting Conversion.* New York: Oxford University Press, 2011.

Tuckett, Christopher. *From the Sayings to the Gospels.* WUNT 328. Tübingen: Mohr Siebeck, 2014.

Tyson, Joseph B. *Marcion and Luke–Acts: A Defining Struggle.* Columbia: University of South Carolina Press, 2006.

Vermes, Geza. *Jesus the Jew.* Philadelphia: Fortress Press, 1973.

Vermez, Geza. *The Authentic Gospel of Jesus.* London: Penguin, 2004.

Wedderburn, J.M. *A History of the First Christians* .London: T&T Clark, 2004.

Williams, Margaret H. *The Jews among the Greeks and Romans: A Diasporan Sourcebook.* John Hopkins University Press, 1998.

Zetterholm, Magnus, ed. *The Messiah in Early Judaism and Christianity.* Minneapolis: Fortress Press, 2007.

Index

Made in the USA
Columbia, SC
19 April 2022

58975393R00107